D0049755

this is not a book about benedict cumberbatch

this is not a book about benedict cumberbatch

the joy of loving something—anything—like your life depends on it

tabitha carvan

G. P. PUTNAM'S SONS
NEW YORK

PUTNAM
— EST. 1838 —
G. P. PUTNAM'S SONS
Publishers Since 1838
An imprint of Penguin Random House LLC
penguinrandomhouse.com

First published in Australia in 2022 by HarperCollins*Publishers*

Library of Congress Control Number: 2022934642

ISBN: 9780593421918
Ebook ISBN: 9780593421925

Printed in the United States of America
1st Printing

For the girls at the concerts

contents

part two

benediction

part three

unencumbered

this is not a book about benedict cumberbatch

preface

What are you thinking about? I am thinking about Benedict Cumberbatch. Even right now (cheekbones), writing this (green-blue-gray eyes), I am (tight-trousered thighs) thinking about (mouth) Benedict Cumberbatch.

I am writing this between thoughts of Benedict Cumberbatch, and I am writing this under photos of Benedict Cumberbatch, including that *Vanity Fair* cover where he has one arm behind his head and the other tugging at the waistband of his trousers. It is the most horizontal that a man could look in a vertical portrait. The photographer, my stand-in, is surely straddling him.

I am writing this from inside Benedict Cumberbatch. His face on a hoodie my husband ordered from the internet for my Christmas present, and which I put on every morning as I tiptoe out of the bedroom to come here. "Do you know how many Benedict Cumberbatch hoodies there are on the internet?" my husband asked me, eyebrow raised, after I unwrapped it. Yes, I do: 3,803.

That's a lot of people inside Benedict Cumberbatch. What are we all doing in there? What am I doing in the spare room, lit only by the laptop's false dawn, while my family sleeps? Why am I, a wife and mother, creeping off in the dark to think about celebrity thighs? Why am I, a grown woman, sticking up pictures of a heartthrob on my wall? Not even in nice frames, but torn out of magazines and stuck on with Blu Tack! It will ruin the paint with greasy stains, like the connect-the-dots pattern I left behind on the walls of my teenage bedroom. Why do I use my precious scraps of free time to watch GIFs animate on a loop, like they're not actually a slightly moving image but a full-length feature movie? A really amazing movie, because I reach the climax every two seconds; that same moment, over and over again, when a man I don't know takes off his scarf. Five stars. Would do again. And again. And again so many more times that I forget to take the bread out of the freezer for school lunches. Later, as I manhandle the contorted icy wads into lunchboxes, I'll tell the kids I'm sure it will be fine by lunchtime.

Will it be fine? Not the sandwiches (no, they definitely won't), but all of it. Me. Will I be fine? I seem to be on the verge of something not right. Whatever this is, it isn't *me*. Soon I'll look straight at the camera and say, "What have I become?" I'll snap out of it. I'll grow up. I'll get to work repainting my walls. I'll say, "Remember the time I was totally obsessed with Benedict Cumberbatch? What was the deal with that?" and everyone will laugh and then I will make the school lunches properly this time.

But my story doesn't seem to be ending this way. Instead of coming to my senses, I come back to the spare room, the photos, the GIFs, the cheekbones. This is very bad news, because I know the only other way the story can end: I embarrass myself. And I am. I'm embarrassing myself, and I'm probably embarrassing you too, with my words like "trousers" and "horizontal." Benedict Cumberbatch himself will be embarrassed, not to mention what-does-your-husband-think-about-all-this.

It's true this doesn't feel like me. Not the me I thought I knew, anyway.

I have never felt so good.

part one

cumberbatched

this is a chapter about mothers

"Ooh, you won't know what's hit you."

The thing about Benedict Cumberbatch is he's ready when you are. He's a gentleman. After you; ladies first.

While it's uncomfortable for me to admit it, Benedict Cumberbatch was standing there holding the door open for me for a very long time. It's not that I didn't notice him, because I absolutely did. During the height of global Cumbermania, c. 2012–2014, it was impossible not to. His strange name. His strange face. *Sherlock* was one of the most watched shows in the world. I remember a phone conversation with my mother, who said Benedict Cumberbatch looked like the underside of a stingray.

Along with his dark, Byronic Sherlock Holmes, he was a jowly blond Yorkshireman in the Tom Stoppard miniseries *Parade's End*; a ginger, secret homosexual with ready access to a hair straightener in *Tinker Tailor Soldier Spy*; a hapless—but singing!—Oklahoman in *August: Osage County*; the "nice" slave owner in *12 Years a Slave*; the "bad" guy in *Star Trek Into Darkness*; Alan Turing in *The Imitation Game*; Julian Assange (I shit you not) in *The Fifth Estate*; and Smaug, a dragon, in *The Hobbit: The Desolation of Smaug*. He famously mispronounced "penguin" as *pengwing* and it went viral; he photobombed U2 at the Oscars and that went viral; he inspired the creation of the online Benedict Cumberbatch Name Generator (Benadryl Cuckooclock, Bentobox Cuttlefish, Burgerking Scratchnsniff . . . honestly, this should just be the rest of the book) and even *that* went viral. He appeared on the cover of *Time* magazine's "Genius Issue"; there was a poem about him in the *London Review of Books*; he even featured in a *New Yorker* cartoon—a pregnant woman is receiving an ultrasound that reveals a cheerful man smiling away in her womb. "Oh, don't worry," the sonographer says. "That's Benedict Cumberbatch. He's in everything." And during all of this, the extent of my thoughts on Benedict Cumberbatch was *Oh, that guy again?* In every role he somehow appeared to be a completely different person, clearing all the data I'd been collecting on what he actually looked like. Every camera angle would reveal a new, planed surface of him, which I could never compose into a whole.

Now, I discuss with other people—many people, many times—their favorite Benedict Cumberbatch parts. Not the parts he plays, you understand. His actual parts. There are the cheekbones (obviously), the nape of his neck, the Cupid's bow of his lip. One woman tells me it's very difficult for her to choose only one and considers her answer for a very long time. She says she believes she could recognize Benedict Cumberbatch from any disembodied fragment of him, "although I might struggle with his ears." I have done an online quiz where you match screenshots of Benedict Cumberbatch's hair with the *Sherlock* episode it appears in, so I could probably do this too. Finally, she settles on her favorite part: the gap between his thumb and forefinger. Ah yes, I say, nodding. That's a really good bit. I know it well.

Benedict Cumberbatch could bring his thumb and forefinger together to show you how small it was, the moment in time that tipped me over from when I couldn't look at him properly to when I couldn't stop looking. Somewhere in that beautiful gap, something changed. He'd been waiting for that moment, uncomplaining, of course, until I was ready. He held the door open, and I walked through. Maybe I brushed against him as I passed. Why not? He's got lots of great parts, after all, and you can do what you want in a metaphor.

But this is what that moment actually looked like: Benedict Cumberbatch is wearing a top hat and pulling on a leather glove. He is in an advertisement for the Victorian-themed *Sherlock* special. The advertisement is in a newspaper, which is lying open on a table in a café, which is where I'm waiting for my takeout coffee. I am drinking coffee because, for the first time in one thousand years, I am neither pregnant nor breastfeeding. I see the ad and I experience a surprising feeling of yearning. I look at that picture, into those eyes that are too far apart on Benedict Cumberbatch's head and yet somehow also perfect, and I think, *Yeah, I reckon I'd like to watch that show.*

I'm sorry this story about such a momentous occasion is so boring, but that's motherhood.

❤

THROUGHOUT MY TWENTIES AND INTO MY THIRTIES, I moved from city to city a fair bit, and wherever I happened to be living, I'd start a blog about it. You need real commitment to get anywhere as a writer, so I was the perfect blogger. I kept a blog about living and studying in Paris when the internet was so new that what I actually had was a "web-log." Then "blog" became a real word, and I wrote one of those, about living in the boho inner west of Sydney. I published it anonymously, and successfully so—when a local newspaper ran a story about it, they assumed the author was a man, and I couldn't have been more pleased. Then I moved to Hanoi for my job and blogged about that, because "blog" was a verb now.

This was where I was living when Benedict Cumberbatch worked his way into the periphery of my consciousness via the debut season of *Sherlock*. The only way for me to watch the show in Vietnam was to buy pirated DVDs from a dusty little shop in the Old Quarter. They had a binder full of DVD covers that you pointed to, as if choosing from a menu, although this was a menu for burning, not cooking. I ordered *Sherlock* and it was served up in a flimsy plastic sleeve.

This was exactly the kind of experience I blogged about, the perspective of the foreigner, for whom even buying a DVD is novel. It made the everyday seem exciting, and people liked it. My blog posts started being republished in newspapers and magazines across Asia and Australia, so I churned out more and more material. Every encounter I had was mined for noteworthiness, and every fleeting incident had inference potential, a broader meaning I could attach my opinion to. I had a lot of opinions.

Then my partner, Nathan, and I got married, I got pregnant, and we moved to Australia's capital, Canberra, for Nathan's job. Nobody wants to read a blog about Canberra, notable only for being neither Sydney nor Melbourne, and located inconveniently in the expanse of country between the two. And besides, I was busy. On my son's birth certificate, it was extremely optimistic of me to declare my profession as "writer." When I did the same thing on my daughter's birth certificate less than two years later, it was straight-up fiction. Which is a kind of writing, I guess?

The dates delineating the cultural phenomenon of Cumbermania—2012 and 2014—are also the years my children were born. Such a short time for a mania, but such a long period of my life. The rest of the world was preoccupied with Benedict Cumberbatch, but I was just preoccupied. There were so many babies, and so many years, and I gave Benedict Cumberbatch as much of my attention as I could spare, which was none. I had nothing to say about him. I had nothing in particular to say about anything. I knew the nap times and feeding times of the children. I knew what was on special at the supermarket. I watched my kids watch birds outside our window. I drank half cups of cold tea. I told my husband stories about what I bought at the supermarket. Pretty good deal on hummus. I had nothing to say about the city I lived in. It seemed fine. The everyday was every day. I drew no inferences.

When you're about to become a mother, people tell you, all the time, "Ooh, you won't know what's hit you!" That makes it sound exciting. I entered motherhood in the brace position waiting for the dramatic crash landing, one where we'd get to go down those inflatable slides and then have a great survivor's story to tell. Maybe I would blog about it! But motherhood doesn't have a moment of impact. Instead, you're stuck in an interminable holding pattern, circling the airport and dumping fuel. And the in-flight entertainment is broken. It just goes on and on, tediously. I was praying for something to hit me, just to break up the monotony.

Things I once thought insignificant now seemed to matter most of all. I could think only of what to make for dinner, of whether the weather was appropriate for drying two loads of washing or three, and it all mattered so much, because there was nothing else, just me and the dinners and the washing and the children. There was no time for anything else. No mental capacity. No emotional availability. No Benedict Cumberbatch.

"Why don't you write anymore?" I would be asked. "Why don't you start a blog again?" Because I have no right. No authority. Nothing interesting. No opinions. No stories. "Nothing happens to me." That's what Dr. Watson tells his therapist in the opening minutes of the first episode of *Sherlock* when he's being encouraged to write a blog. And then the theme music starts so you know something is about to happen to him. Nothing happened to me. There was no theme music. It was so long since I'd listened to any music at all that our household had changed music-playing systems and I didn't even bother to find out how to operate the new one.

I am writing this as if I knew what was going on, or was even reflecting upon it at the time, but that is all hindsight. Then, it was just one day after another, tolerable only for not questioning it. I read *Alice's Adventures in Wonderland* to my children at bedtime, but I didn't even register anything of the conversation between Alice and the Caterpillar when she tells him she can't explain herself because she's not herself. I read that to my children, and I didn't scream and sob and tear out the page and say, *This! I am not myself!* and circle it madly using all the red pens I could find in the house. I said, "That's enough for tonight," and then I closed the book. I was in too many pieces to process such thoughts, or to attend wholly to them. Wholly!—an impossible idea. The cup of tea was not whole, the alphabet puzzle was not whole, the pelvic floor was not whole, the night was not whole, and I most of all, I was not whole.

I never knew Kierkegaard was funny, but I think this is funny: "The greatest hazard of all, losing one's self, can occur very quietly in the world, as if it were nothing at all. No other loss can occur so quietly; any other loss—an arm, a leg, five dollars, a wife, etc.—is sure to be noticed." I did not notice. I would catch my reflection in the mirror in the bathroom, where I went again and again to wash my hands after changing diapers. So used to gazing down at babies, I was shocked, every time, to discover there was another face up there. Our eyes would meet, and then I would finish drying my red, cracked hands and leave her behind, as if she were nothing at all. I guess it's not that funny.

It might sound like I had postpartum depression. Later—much, much later—I would write about these years of my life in a story that was posted to an online parenting group. I watched as the group's mothers and mothers-to-be debated whether I was depressed. "Surely this is mental illness!" someone would comment, only to be matched by someone else commenting, "But this is just normal!" I witnessed my best friend go through terrible postpartum depression during the same period and by comparison, I saw I was absolutely fine. Functional, lucky. Happy, even.

For the years I was either pregnant or breastfeeding, I was simply hostage to my chemistry, the hormones that kept me feeling permanently, steadily absorbed. They directed my focus to the children at the expense of all else. Like, you know, independent thought. A free spirit. It was not until the second baby was finally weaned, and I discovered that the brand of tampon I used for the last time four years previous had gone out of business, that I realized I had been in captivity.

Well, I say "realized," but it was Benedict Cumberbatch who told me.

When I was pregnant, I goaded my mother into talking about the pain of childbirth, and she told me a story that also involves mirrors. She said, matter-of-factly, that giving birth is so painful you feel you've been torn in two. "They should put mirrors in the labor ward," she advised, as if putting it in a suggestion box. "So you can see you've not been broken into pieces." I wondered later if my mother was recalling the pain of labor or actually everything that comes after, because later I understood that is exactly what motherhood is. The "shattering" is what the writer Sarah Manguso calls it in her *Harper's* essay about writing and mothering: the "disintegration of the self, after which the original form is quite gone."

When the haze of hormones, chronic sleeplessness, and alcohol-free nights lifted, I finally knew what had hit me. I looked around for pieces of myself I recognized, and tried to put the component parts back together, but nothing fit the same way anymore. The original form was quite gone. The new composition I made in its place was rough-hewn, with exposed cracks and gaps. That's how Benedict Cumberbatch found a way in. He squeezed my heart, he rattled my bones, he tapped out a message in Morse code on my rib cage: *Who are you?*

❤

WHAT CAME FIRST: THE CHICKEN OR THE EGGS BENE-dict? Correlation or causation; Sherlock Holmes would have something to say about that. Did something essential about Benedict Cumberbatch inspire my desire? Or did he just happen to be there when I was ready to feel it, a case of right place, right time, right top hat? I can only tell you that all of a sudden, a person I'd seen one hundred times before looked different after one hundred and one. I can only say that feelings I'd previously labeled as the malformed offcuts of adolescent development caught my eye from the discard pile, and they sparkled like new. Something lurched into motion in the pit of my belly, that churning, squeezing madness for more that leaves you in no doubt why they call it a "crush." *Oh!* I thought, remembering how it feels. And then, immediately, my next thought: *It feels so good.*

I put the kids to bed, plonked myself on the couch, and watched the Victorian-themed special of *Sherlock*. I watched Sherlock Holmes and Dr. Watson solving a Gothic mystery about a ghost bride. The game's afoot; elementary, my dear Watson; and so on. I watched all of that, but really what I did was ogle. And look, honestly, that doesn't fully capture what was going on, shall we say, *internally*. Columnist for the *Times* Caitlin Moran once drunk-tweeted while watching *Sherlock* that she would like to climb Benedict Cumberbatch "like a tree." "I would do him until Security pulled me off—then wank at him from behind a door." I was neither drunk nor tweeting, and that is very much for the best. As soon as *Sherlock* finished, I wanted to watch it again. Again! What a waste of my time that would be!

Radical thoughts for new mothers: you feel a feeling all of

your own. Total subversion: you act on it, just because you want to.

I watched that episode of *Sherlock* once more. Then I watched all the other episodes. Or, I should say, I watched them *again*, because I had actually seen them all before, but they were completely different now. Benedict Cumberbatch looked completely different. All the parts of his face fitted together perfectly. Now, just the sight of his face would make my heart beat faster. Pulse: elevated; pupils: dilated. My lips would involuntarily bend into a smile when I thought about him. Like I'm smiling now, because that line about the pulse and the pupils is ripped straight from *Sherlock*, a scene where Benedict Cumberbatch might be at his absolute hottest. I would make excuses to talk about him, to read about him, to look at him, in exactly the same way I have done in the past for crushes, diverting my daily routine to "casually" pass by their house, always finding one more reason to get back in touch, to hit play again.

I watched all of his interviews on YouTube. Then I watched everything, all of it, again. I watched him while the children napped. I conducted endless searches of him in Google Images with one hand while rolling toy cars around on the floor with the other. I listened to him on my phone, a background purr while making dinner. When the children were in bed, I made Nathan watch Benedict Cumberbatch's entire back catalog, one night after the other, including an interminable movie where he plays William Pitt the Younger, and also a whole series set in the early nineteenth century where Benedict Cumberbatch is on a ship. There's one scene where you get to see his Cumberbottom.

It was in South Africa, during the filming of that ship series, that Benedict Cumberbatch and two of his fellow actors were carjacked and (briefly) kidnapped. He discusses the incident repeatedly in interviews, always with the epilogue that afterward he went skydiving, drove his motorbike faster, and felt more and differently alive. With the same spirit of adventure, I went out drinking. (It's like skydiving for mothers recently retired from breastfeeding.) I made the three-hour bus trip to Sydney alone—alone!—and went straight to a bar to meet a friend I've known for a long time.

My friend doesn't want children, and he'd watched his circle of friends drop off the radar, one by one, as they started their families. "I thought I had lost you," he said. I agreed it was a close call, that I had almost lost myself too. We raised our glasses to the future. Then I drank too many espresso martinis and talked too much, too quickly, about Benedict Cumberbatch. My friend asked for clarification: "Wait, what—the guy with the face?"

On our way to another bar, strutting down the nighttime city street, I felt electric, but also like every minute we spent not talking about Benedict Cumberbatch was agony. I shoved my phone under my friend's nose to show him images of Benedict Cumberbatch, no different from a new parent subjecting him to unwanted slide shows of their baby. I had saved so many photos of Benedict Cumberbatch that my phone's facial recognition algorithm knew who he was and had sorted him automatically into his own album, right alongside those for my children. My friend scrutinized the photos, squinting, like he was trying to identify a suspect wanted for a crime. If, earlier in the evening, he'd been relieved to discover he hadn't lost me to motherhood, he was no doubt now realizing he'd lost me to something even more unrelatable.

He shook his head, exasperated. "I don't get it."

The thing about fantasy is it can't be observed in reality. This makes it fun but also the symptom of a mental health disorder. When I went to bed that night, I was too caffeinated to sleep, and too annoyed. I seethed at how my friend had dismissed—so casually!—something that mattered so much. What would he even know?

"This is important to me," Sherlock Holmes says to John Watson in that *Sherlock* special, talking about a case. "No," John replies firmly. "This is you needing a fix." I lay in bed and scrolled through the photos on my phone until all I was thinking about was Benedict Cumberbatch. The tap-tap-tap of his question reverberated through my bones. *Who. Are. You.*

I didn't know what to say.

chapter two

this is a chapter about obsessions

"Are we looking at the same dude?
What the frick?!"

My obsession with Benedict Cumberbatch barely had time to get going before I felt a twinge of terror. In contrast to the way I unquestioningly accepted the stultifications of early motherhood, I entered the Benedict Cumberbatch years knowing full well that *something* was happening to me, and that it probably wasn't okay. Like, just now, I considered referring to "the Benedict Cumberbatch years" as "the BC era" but then I thought, *No, it's probably not okay to liken him to the Son of God,* even though Benedict Cumberbatch is absolutely the first thing that comes to mind when I see those initials, and also the first thing that comes to mind when I think about God, gods, demigods, God-given gifts, and holy mother of God, now you've really got me going on Benedict Cumberbatch.

We're not too different from those famous pleasure-loving lab rats, wired up to a lever that stimulated their brain's reward center. Some of those rats "self-stimulated" as often as two thousand times an hour for twenty-four hours and had to be disconnected from the apparatus to stop them starving themselves to death. I could look at an image of Benedict Cumberbatch and practically hear my pleasure receptors pinging in approval. It was terrifyingly effective. I craved new content all the time, wanting Benedict Cumberbatch in front of my eyeballs whenever and wherever possible. I found it difficult to find other uses for my paws. I imagine it's the same for porn addicts, searching deeper and deeper within the internet to fulfill their more and more specific and hard-core proclivities, except I was plumbing the very depths of BBC historical dramas.

I did not want to be disconnected from the apparatus—no, I wanted to keep looking at Benedict Cumberbatch!—but I also wanted to avoid ending up at a Not-Traditionally-Good-Looking-Yet-Extremely-Attractive-Celebrities Anonymous meeting, sitting next to some Steve Buscemi fan, having to declare I was an addict. I knew I should police myself to keep my burgeoning addiction in check, the way we have all learned to do with our sad little tricks for controlling our mobile phone usage, but I didn't know where to begin. I couldn't even really understand what this addiction actually was. I certainly hadn't heard of it happening to anyone else. "Thirsty, but only for water taken from one particular well," in the words of Balzac, a man who understood thirst long before Urban Dictionary did. "Cathexis," according to Freud: the concentration of mental or emotional energy on a particular person, idea, or object, to a possibly unhealthy degree.

I learned that top-shelf word from a Tumblr user calling herself Professor Fangirl, writing about Benedict Cumberbatch: "I have an erotic cathexis on this particular man, on the aggregate of his appearance, the characters he plays, the way he performs, and on the few facts I know about his life." Hard same, Professor. But I wouldn't read that until later. I didn't know yet that people were writing things like this. I hadn't met my first Cumberbitch. I still thought that my experience, unique in its specificity and unprecedented in its intensity, could only be happening to me and me alone. I laugh at the memory of this. It's like when I got my first period and my reaction was commensurate with it being the first period that anyone in the whole history of the world had ever experienced. Standing in our bathroom, my mother resorted to listing off every woman who has ever menstruated—"Your sisters! Your cousins! Your aunts! Kylie Minogue! The *queen*!"—to try to budge me, using the sheer force of data, from the center of my universe. I would have to go through this same process again, but this time with Benedict Cumberbatch. I would have to discover, yet again, that I was in sync with more women than I ever could have imagined.

But until then, I remained freaked out; very quietly, very privately, but still completely freaked out. I knew that if I voiced anything of what I was thinking, it would sound straight-up bad. My husband, Nathan, had clocked that something was going on, obviously, since our evening's viewing schedule was being determined by Benedict Cumberbatch's IMDb page like it was the actual TV guide. But as would become apparent later—when the words "It's just a show" would kick off the biggest meltdown our marriage had ever seen—he didn't understand the extent of it. At all. I wasn't about to explain to him, or anyone, that I just needed some time to myself to cathect. And if we can't—or don't want to—name something, label it, and put it into a box, it's difficult to know how to present it, and even more difficult to know how to receive it.

Recently, a colleague of mine commented that he believed my love of Benedict Cumberbatch to be an "ironic" kind of love. This colleague sits right next to my desk, which for a long time now has been covered in Benedict Cumberbatch paraphernalia, including a card he very sweetly bought for me that says—possibly in violation of HR policy—*I'll be the Benedict in your Cumberbatch.* "What do you think all this is, then?" I said, waving my arms to indicate the display, but I understood why he'd come to that conclusion. That it's tongue-in-cheek performance art seems more likely, and more palatable, than the alternative: that the grown woman occupying this desk is . . . addicted to . . . looking at . . . a man's face? Is suffering from some kind of tragic mental and emotional regression? Has untamed libidinous urges that she's discharging right here in her cubicle? Better not to talk about it, really.

I'm going to try to do a better job now than I did then of

explaining how I felt. I want you to get it. I even filled out a questionnaire for you, something called the "Celebrity Attitude Scale" from a psychology journal. It determines the extent of "celebrity worship syndrome" based on twenty-three statements with which to agree or disagree. For example, Item 20 reads: *If someone gave me several thousand dollars to do with as I please, I would consider spending it on a personal possession (like a napkin or paper plate) once used by my favorite celebrity.* Strongly disagree! How ridiculous! Benedict Cumberbatch would always make sure to dispose of his rubbish properly. (See Item 16: *I often feel compelled to learn the personal habits of my favorite celebrity.*)

After filling it all out, I find I am an "intense-personal" celebrity worshipper, meaning I identify strongly with, and obsess about, my chosen celebrity. But I already know this, and you already know this, and how does this diagnosis even begin to help you understand what I was actually feeling? (Item 2: *I share with my favorite celebrity a special bond that cannot be described in words.*) I guess it does tell you that I'm not a "borderline-pathological" celebrity worshipper. I'm not Eminem's deranged fan, Stan, from the song of the same name, or the stalker who shot Ronald Reagan to impress Jodie Foster. I'm not writing to you from inside prison. In response to Item 1 on the Celebrity Attitude Scale—*If I were to meet my favorite celebrity in person, he/she would already somehow know that I am his/her biggest fan*—I said "strongly disagree"! As if! It's not like I wrote a book about him or anything!

So I hunted around in other academic studies to find you a more meaningful description. One said celebrity worship is associated with criminality; another said it's associated with "maladaptive daydreaming" and "problematic internet use" (pfft, like there's any other kind); another revealed that the words most associated with celebrity worshippers are "irresponsible," "subordinate," and "foolish." There was also a study of a fan club devoted to aging British crooner Cliff Richard, which reports that despite members treating him like a god, "most view Cliff as human." I couldn't tell if that was irresponsible, subordinate, or foolish. None of these articles felt like they were about me. I didn't connect with them at all. I was, however, compelled by one study to measure the length of my second and fourth fingers. Just like the study says it would, my digit ratio suggests a propensity for celebrity worship. Apparently it also indicates a willingness to believe in superstitions and the paranormal, so this finger voodoo seems totally legit.

I wish I could use my magical fingers to point to an example, a common reference, that would help you to get it. I wish you knew my birdwatching friend Simon (or maybe you do, in which case, who's the creepy stalker now, eh?), because then I could say, *You know how whenever you're talking to Simon, he's paying attention to you and saying "Uh-huh" at all the appropriate moments, but his eyes are always trained slightly above your head and occasionally he'll just leap up with a pair of binoculars, even when you're sitting indoors?* And you'd say, *Yes! Classic Simon!* and then I'd say that's how I feel about

Benedict Cumberbatch, like he's always close to hand, even in impossible circumstances, if only I remain alert to the possibility. Or maybe if you knew my friend Nigel, then we could remember together the time he bought tickets to every single Leonard Cohen concert on the singer's last tour of Australia. And how I said to him, when I bumped into him at the park, where he was—this actually happened—reading a book of Leonard Cohen poetry, "But what if the concerts aren't any good?" and Nigel replied with a disgusted noise and said, "Would a Christian worry that the Second Coming might be a letdown?" And I thought, *Well, maybe, if Christ had written a song as bad as "Jazz Police,"* but I said nothing because in that moment, I understood that Nigel's unassailable devotion to Leonard Cohen did not come from a place of reason or logic. That's like me and Benedict Cumberbatch.

But then you would say that these stories tell you nothing about an obsession with Benedict Cumberbatch because the wholesome pastimes of birdwatching and musical appreciation are not analogous to perving on an actual, living human man. And I would be forced to agree. Because even though it would be very convenient to say it's just like birdwatching but swap the birds for Benedict Cumberbatch, there's something othering about obsessions that makes them impossible to line up and compare. I once went birdwatching with Simon. We had to get up earlier than I had ever imagined possible, and then sit perfectly still, quiet and cold among some bushes in a Vietnamese national park, while Simon grew increasingly anxious about seeing or not seeing some very specific small brown bird that appeared to me to be identical to any other small brown bird. I could only manage to hold in my mind sustained, focused thoughts about that bird for about eight seconds at a time and then I would start to fantasize about the sandwiches we'd packed but seemingly had no intention of unwrapping. I grew so hungry that when I think about that trip now, over ten years later, what comes to mind first, and vividly, is the eventual, glorious satiation of that sandwich, which was a chewy baguette smeared with Laughing Cow cheese. I can't remember, nor do I even care, if we saw that bird.

So, sure, I have an obsession, but it's not like *that*. For starters, that bird was very boring and Benedict Cumberbatch is very interesting.

But if not like *that*, then like what? I borrowed a book from the library called *Obsession: A History* in search of precedents and cultural contexts to present to you as evidence that obsessions are not new, nor deviant, but perfectly respectable and explainable. Highbrow, even! I got that Balzac quote from that book, and I planned for there to be many more tidbits like that to present to you with an impressive flourish. Do you know about Lisztomania, for example—the fan hysteria for the pianist Franz Liszt that swept through Europe in the 1840s? His szwooning female admirers would turn his broken piano strings into bracelets, or carry glass vials containing dregs of his coffee. One woman encased one of Liszt's old cigar butts in a locket encrusted with diamonds spelling out "FL"—it's the nineteenth-century equivalent of paying several thousand dollars on eBay for a discarded napkin!

But *Obsession: A History* didn't turn out to be an edifying source. Quite the opposite. On page two, the author shares a personal anecdote to demonstrate his affinity with the obsessives he studies, as if saying, *We're not that different, you and I!* but I'm afraid it did not have the desired effect. When he was a child, the author confides in us, he compulsively swallowed coins. Mostly pennies and dimes, but nickels as well. He pursued this obsession, he says, for "the subsequent visual delight of seeing these gleaming circles emerge from me shiny and cleaned by the acid of my digestive system." Look, that's perfectly fine, absolutely fine, completely fine, but my obsession is not like *that*.

I'm sure Nigel and Simon are now feeling the same way reading this: *please don't drag us and our totally reasonable interests into whatever weird thing you've got going on with Benedict Cumberbatch like they're somehow the same.* This is just how obsessions seem to work. Our own obsessions are exquisite; they're the gleaming circles that encompass, perfectly, our innermost thoughts and desires. But when we turn our insides out to display them to the world, expose these precious, private parts of ourselves to the light, all anyone else sees is a toilet bowl full of poo coins.

It doesn't actually matter if you don't like Benedict Cumberbatch or don't see the appeal. Maybe you'd choose the poo coins over him. That's okay, everyone likes different things, and it means if you and I are ever in the same room with Benedict Cumberbatch you can just wave him through to me. "He's all yours," you can say, and it won't get awkward between us.

I know from experience that it's not a conversion you can force. There's an *SNL* sketch about this, where contestants, including special guest Benedict Cumberbatch, compete in a game show called "Why Is Benedict Cumberbatch Hot?" After listening to the female contestants answer the titular question by making a series of lewd, horny noises, the male game show host cries out in frustration, "Are we looking at the same dude? What the frick?!" Benedict Cumberbatch himself then agrees that it's very confusing. It *is* confusing, like we *aren't* looking at the same dude, like I'm looking at Benedict Cumberbatch through heart-shaped binoculars. He only exists for me in that place that connects us, the looker and the looked at. And now you—the looky-loo—are in there too, killing the mood a bit, I have to say, so I at least have to try to explain myself, even if I can't explain *him*.

I need to find someone who knows exactly what I'm talking about, someone who'll say, "I hear you!" and I can say, "See! I might be crazy, but I'm not alone." I need to speak to Vanessa. She's a fanfiction author who has been writing and publishing installments of the same single story on the fanfiction platform Archive of Our Own, over a period of *eight years*. It's about Benedict Cumberbatch: a fictionalized version of his real-life biography starting from when he became famous. Last I checked, it was clocking in at 1,807,687 words, over 224 chapters, making it three times the length of *War and Peace*. It's not completed yet. Vanessa is making a life's work out of her obsession, so she will clearly understand mine, piddling as it is by comparison.

I send her an email, asking to speak to her about how her obsession has managed to generate such intense focus and dedication. I want to ask her how she would describe her state of mind. Where does she sit on the Celebrity Attitude Scale? Does she ever worry that her obsession is compulsive? I mean, we're talking 1.8 *million* words here. If you stacked copies of the book you're currently reading, one on top of the other, you'd need thirty of them to match the size of her—unfinished—work.

Vanessa doesn't write back agreeing to be interviewed. She replies with a question for me instead: "Why do you use the word 'obsession'? To me, the word has an almost negative connotation." *Yes, well, exactly,* I think, scrunching up my nose as I go over her response again. I'm baffled. If it's not an obsession, what else could it be?

chapter three

this is a chapter about fear

"I can handle good, but I don't know what to do with *too* good."

Awhile ago I was at a writing event, mingling at cocktail hour with other aspiring authors. Many of them were writing extremely important and worthy books about things like surviving abusive relationships or overcoming trauma. I found myself gulping down red wine and off-loading the same introduction onto every single one of them: "I'm writing a book about how I fell in love with Benedict Cumberbatch HAHAHAHAHA." I wanted to make sure they knew I was in on the joke. It seemed natural to me—no, it's more than that—it seemed *necessary* to me to recognize the not-rightness of my obsession; to get in first and acknowledge that it is, in Vanessa's words, "almost negative" HAHAHAHAHA.

As I was making my way through the room in this fashion, I met a woman who was writing a book about her career as a jockey. After my deranged introduction about Benedict

Cumberbatch, she just said, calmly, "Yeah, I get that. It's like women and horses." I looked at her, with her black leather boots and long, thick hair, and thought, *I have no idea what this horsey woman is talking about.* Benedict Cumberbatch once said in a Q&A that the worst insult ever leveled at him was "arse-named, horse-faced," but this was the only connection between the two subjects I could make. Horsey girls have always been very confusing to me. Probably noticing my expression, she explained: "It's about finding a way to lose control." I nodded and drank more wine. *But,* I thought, *why would someone* want *to lose control? Especially of a horse!* I continued to have no idea what she meant until much later, when I met Kyndall. Actually, I didn't properly understand for a long time even after that. It just sounded to me like she wasn't a very good jockey.

♥

KYNDALL, FIFTY-FIVE, IS SPEAKING FROM HER HOME office in Ohio. She's got the classic "neutral" background for a video call: the filing cabinets, the family photo, the documents pinned to the corkboard. There's a large picture of a dandelion puff on the wall. I was given her contact details by a mutual acquaintance who had said, during a conversation about obsessions getting out of hand, "You have *got* to speak to my friend Kyndall." Nothing is getting out of hand here, as far as I can see.

Kyndall tells me she used to be a horsey girl. "At one point my entire room was plastered with horse pictures. I drew horses, I had model horses. Actually, for almost a year when I was very young, I lived on all fours." She smiles. She has one of those genuine grins that is so broad that it doesn't so much dimple her cheeks as take over her whole face. "I would go up and down the stairs on all fours, pretending I was a horse. I wore a tail and had little jumping competitions where I would run around on all fours and jump over jumps I made in the house. My parents were probably very worried."

Eventually, Kyndall stands up on two feet, and then she gets herself real horses to ride in real competitions. She loves horses so much she wants to become a horse trainer, but when she turns eighteen and the time comes to make a decision about college, she says goodbye to the horses and chooses accounting. "It was the sensible option," she says. Being sensible is in Kyndall's DNA. Her mom, a bookkeeper, would patch bath towels instead of buying new ones, even though money wasn't tight. "We never took a vacation as a family, ever. I think we went to a state park once that was like an hour away. It was all about thrift." From when she was thirteen, Kyndall helped her mom with the books for the family's plumbing business, so she is familiar with accounting. Plus, she figures she could make a lot of money.

After graduating from college, Kyndall dresses in gray suits and drives a gray Honda because she wants to be a businesswoman and this is how they look. "I was always so concerned about just being this successful, conservative accountant." When she's twenty-two, her future husband spots her in the cafeteria near where they both work. He points her out to his friend and says, "I'm going to marry a girl like *that*." She's wearing a starched white button-down shirt with a little tie, a long plaid pleated skirt, and a blazer. Kyndall has a great mass of curly hair, perfectly unruly, just like you see in ads for conditioner. I bet she looked great.

The thing about "dressing for the job you want" works for Kyndall. By the time she's forty, she is vice president of a global public company. "I have kids. I have a husband. And I work: crazy hours, stressful job. That was my identity: I was a successful female executive. My work was my life. It was my singular focus."

Despite the stress, she enjoys her job and, just like she had hoped, she makes a lot of money. "I mean, *a lot*. Like, four times more than my husband and he's got a good job." But the money doesn't make her flashy. Her colleagues have house cleaners and drive fancy cars and get pedicures, but she does none of that. "I remember at a meeting there was a lady sitting next to me and I said, 'Oh, I like your shoes.' And she said, 'Yeah, I just bought these. I got a really good deal on them: $350.' And I thought, 'I got mine for $20 and they look just like yours.' That's smarter."

Instead of spending her money, Kyndall saves as much of it as she can. She does this, she says, to keep her options open. "I was constantly in fear that I was going to be fired at any moment. I didn't want to lose my house or be eating out of garbage cans if that happened. People would tell me I was good at my job, but I could never see that myself. I would think, 'I've fooled you too.'" In her mind, she just *looks* like a successful accountant, as if it's very convincing cosplay.

Kyndall works most weekends. She doesn't have close friends or any time for hobbies, but this doesn't bother her. It's a long drive from her home to her workplace on the other side of Columbus—sometimes taking two hours each way if the weather's bad—but this is where she's always lived, her entire life, so she doesn't think of moving. On the plus side, her long commute constitutes her "free time," during which she listens to audiobooks in the car. She chooses long books because they're the best value for money. That's smarter.

After her youngest daughter leaves home for college, freeing up some more time and mental space in her life, Kyndall decides she'd better see a psychologist. Normally she wouldn't want to spend money on something like that, but both her daughters have ADHD, and they'd gotten her thinking she could have some kind of obsessive disorder. She'd let her work completely take over her life, after all.

But that's not why she needs a psychologist. Nope, her career is not the problem at all. In fact, her job is everything she'd always hoped for; her life story is playing out exactly as she scripted it. She's booking an appointment at the psychologist's because something else, something totally unexpected, is now getting in the way of her job. Which is quite scary when your work is your life.

"I would be at work and more and more I was thinking, 'Oh my God, do I really want to do tax returns?'" she explains.

(I know this is hard to get your head around, but *not* wanting to do tax returns is what's ringing alarm bells for Kyndall.) At the psychologist's, she elaborates on her situation. "I just have this abundance of weird energy. I guess you could even describe it as sexual energy. What is happening to me?" she asks. "I'm going crazy. I'm going insane. All I want to do is write stories and make art. . . ."

She pauses in the retelling, her eyes lighting up. "Did you know I do art?" she asks. I didn't. "Can I show you?" she says, and she shares her screen to reveal a digital painting of Benedict Cumberbatch as Sherlock Holmes, dressed in a lavender bra, semi-sheer panties, and suspenders. The only other thing he's wearing is a touch of purple eye shadow and a flick of eyeliner. Maybe he's dressing for the job he wants too. He's seated, one hand posed just below his hip, his legs in a straddle. Under his pale thighs, you can see a hint of what might be sheepskin. It's a good painting! I note the impressive accuracy in the placement of Benedict Cumberbatch's neck freckles.

You know what's a really long audiobook? *The Adventures of Sherlock Holmes.* I bet you can work out the rest of what happened from there.

Back at the psychologist's, Kyndall continues: "I'm obsessed with this TV show. I'm in love with Sherlock. It's totally out of control." She is here, making her first-ever visit to a mental health professional, because she wants to be cured. "I want to be diagnosed with something and to take some kind of medication that will stop me feeling like I am insane. I want to feel normal again. I want to go back to my normal life."

Becoming obsessed with a TV character is not sensible, and being out of control feels scary. Like, let's-go-to-the-psychologist-for-a-diagnosis kind of scary. This is understandable since, historically speaking, going out of control has not usually panned out well, especially for women. Since the fifth century BC—yep, that's right, *BC*—we've had a name for what happens when women go out of control: hysteria. It was the ancient Egyptians who decided this was all to do with the uterus. Specifically, and also literally, a uterus that doesn't know its place. In the Ebers Papyrus, we can read the cure for an uppity uterus, which is the placement of malodorous substances near the woman's mouth. If you have a downity uterus, you put the malodorous substances near the vagina. And it was by maneuvering the uterus thus, a little bit this way, then a little bit that way, that the ancient Egyptians invented the spirit level. No wonder the pyramids turned out so well!

Over time, as the centuries passed, you could thankfully count on the uterus to stay wherever you last saw it, but it continued to be perceived as A Womb with a Mood. "Uterine fury," an excellent term coined by the Romans, was a diagnosis you could find yourself with up until the Middle Ages. This condition was observable in women suffering from lovesickness, exhibiting a loss of control and decorum. In his *Treatise on Lovesickness* from 1623, the physician Jacques Ferrand says uterine fury is characterized by "excessive burning desire in the womb" causing the afflicted to "chatter incessantly and speak about, or like to hear about, sexual matters." The cure is moral correction, specifically marital sex. More effective than a cure, though, is the prophylactic measure, which can stop a uterus before it gets completely out of hand: the threat of public shaming. Shaming women out of having weird sexual energy! Those seventeenth-century physicians with their zany ideas.

About four hundred years later, Kyndall presents herself to the psychologist with, let's face it, an absolutely *furious* uterus. Her own internalized spirit level is telling her something is completely out of whack. I'm sorry, but just briefly, I have to also tell you about this part in Daniel Bergner's *What Do Women Want?*, where he writes about the development of a drug to increase libido in women, like a female version of Viagra. He quotes a scientist who's conducting one of these drug trials as saying: "You want your effects to be good but not too good." That's the ideal for female desire: good but not *too* good. Otherwise, Bergner reports, we might end up with "female excesses, crazed binges of infidelity, societal splintering."

Kyndall feels like she's heading straight toward this Girls Gone Wild end-times scenario. It's all too much. She tells the psychologist she doesn't know "where to put all the energy" being generated by these new feelings. One night, she gets out of bed and writes an erotic story based on the characters from *Sherlock*. "I've never written anything in my entire life, but I write this story in the middle of the night.

The next morning I get up, I read it and think, 'Well, that's not bad.'"

Then she starts to draw too. "When I was younger, I used to draw all the time, but I hadn't drawn for decades." She connects with other fans on Twitter and discovers all these other people, many of them women in their fifties just like her, writing fanfiction and creating fanart. This only increases her energy levels and creative urges, and now she's thinking about it "all the time."

More than that, she's thinking thoughts a sensible person simply does not have. "I am starting to think that I want to leave my job. Just walk away." She does the math and works out that she's saved enough money to retire immediately. "I am just so unsettled. I am unsatisfied. I really feel nuts. And all of a sudden I have this incredible sex drive too, which feels like it's intertwined with the mental episode." She's frank with the psychologist about this. Previously happy with her sex life, now Kyndall can't get enough. "My poor husband!" she says. "You might think, 'Gosh, he's lucky,' but he was not happy. He was not on board." Maybe the people doing those female Viagra trials were right.

Kyndall wants to forget about the purple lingerie and get back to the business suits, because she believes that her "normal" self is the accountant. Again, this is understandable, because when we think of our best, authentic self, we see someone who's self-disciplined, practicing impulse control. It's an idea we've borrowed from the popular narrative of recovery and addiction, writes the sociologist Helen Keane in *What's Wrong with Addiction?* Being in control is held up as "an ideal of health" meaning that "deviation from it becomes a disease or disorder that requires remedy." This is where Kyndall is at. She wants a remedy. But it's not what she's going to get.

"So, what did the psychologist say?" I ask her.

"She had a checklist and she went through it, asking questions about whether all of these new feelings were affecting my functioning. And when she reached the end of her checklist, she said, 'You're fine.'"

"Just like that? 'You're fine'?"

"She said, 'You're passionate. It sounds like you've found a passion, a hobby.'"

"Wow, okay," I say. This is not what I thought was going to happen. I was certain Kyndall was going to be told her obsession, while not diagnosable, was still a cry for help of some kind.

"She's telling you that this is normal, that you're not crazy?"

"Yes, and I was very disappointed to hear that," Kyndall says.

When you have eliminated the impossible, whatever remains, however improbable, must be the truth. (It's up to you whether you want to imagine Sherlock Holmes wearing sexy lingerie while he's saying that.) Kyndall knows if she's of sound mind, that can only mean one thing. She must want this. She wants to be out of control.

She came for answers and is leaving with even more

questions. What does it *mean* to want this? Did she want this all along? Who was she all this time, and who is she now? And what is she supposed to wear? After the consultation, Kyndall imagines the psychologist is laughing about her. "I wasted this woman's time with my stupid problems when she's probably got suicidal people or people with real mental health problems coming in. And I'm just horny and I like *Sherlock*." She huffs out a laugh at the ridiculousness of it, at how something so small can feel so big.

When something as benign as a hobby—a *hobby!*—comes to feel transgressive, what has gone wrong there? Why does an objectively good thing, like a new passion, trigger an identity crisis? It's not going to be in the *DSM*, sure, but when a woman feels pleasure and then promptly goes to a psychologist to ask for it to be taken away, that seems like, I don't know, *something*. "My whole life has been motivated by fear. I think that's the thing," Kyndall says.

I sigh. I can only agree HAHAHAHAHA. I am also afraid. Afraid of being judged, of embarrassing myself. I'm afraid of feeling too good. I can handle good, but I don't know what to do with *too* good. And I'd rather call myself crazy or deflect the question with a joke at my own expense than have to work out why that is.

If I could say my obsession is a kinky sex thing, or a mental episode brought on by a hormonal imbalance, or a cry for help revealing some big underlying problem, then the enormity of the feelings it has generated in me would make sense. The punishment would fit the crime, so to speak. It would be like those intentionally shocking first-person essays that the website xoJane used to run in their IT HAPPENED TO ME section. They actually did publish one called "IT HAPPENED TO ME: I Became So Obsessed with Benedict Cumberbatch That I Was Sure We'd Get Married." To give you an idea of just how bad an obsession with Benedict Cumberbatch is assumed to be, they also ran an essay called "IT HAPPENED TO ME: My Gynecologist Found a Ball of Cat Hair in My Vagina." These essays always end with a lesson that transforms the ordeal into something valuable: it's better to live in reality than fantasy; don't let your cat sleep on your bed (or at least I *think* that was the lesson). But if my obsession isn't a shocking aberration, if it doesn't exist to teach me a moral, if it is, in fact, just a measly hobby, then I'm left with this: "IT HAPPENED TO ME: I Found Something I Like and Now I Don't Know Who I Am Anymore." What the hell kind of story is that?

I end the call and sit in silence for a moment with the realization that maybe I'm not writing the book I thought I was. I was trying so hard to make you get it, but I don't think I even got it myself. I wish my feelings about Benedict Cumberbatch really were a joke, because that would be much easier, but I'm sorry to say they actually mean a great deal to me. I think about how long it's been since I felt this way, since I had a passion. I don't know about you, but for me, it's been so long that I didn't even notice anything was missing from my life. Is that what being in control looks like? Is it just about not wanting something enough?

In Helen Keane's book about addiction, she says we have to leave room for the idea that ambiguous experiences can be valuable. "Feelings of dislocation, of fragmentation and unreality," she writes, "can be sought after as life-enhancing or transformative as well as being evidence of disease and disorder." Being in control is not the same as being free; and being out of control isn't always scary. Or maybe it is scary, but good-scary.

Apparently, in Hebrew there are many words for "fear," although it's possible this is not entirely true, like the thing about Inuit and "snow." In any case, according to the self-described "Zen rabbi" Alan Lew, there's one Hebrew translation for "fear," *norah*, which is more like what we'd call awe or exhilaration. He defines it as "the fear that overcomes us when we suddenly find ourselves in possession of considerably more energy than we are used to, inhabiting a larger space than we are used to inhabiting." A small thing becomes big.

An email comes through from Kyndall. It's a photo. During our call, I had noticed her eyes roaming above her screen, and, often, to make a point, she would gesture to something on the wall behind her computer, which I couldn't see. I asked her if she could send me a photo of what she was looking at, her view of our conversation. You know when you're wandering around IKEA, looking at the little pretend rooms, and it's all Scando birch and expanses of white laminate, and then you get to the one room that's crammed with a million pictures in black fames and mix-matched patterned furnishings, and you can't help but gasp? That's what Kyndall's desk setup looks like. A section of the wall has been covered with the same busy wallpaper print that appears in 221B Baker Street, and hanging on it, and on every spare inch of the rest of the wall, there are *Sherlock* posters, postcards, fanart illustrations, signed photos of Benedict Cumberbatch, a floor plan of 221B, a deerstalker cap, a leather riding crop, and a pair of red underpants (a reference to a long-running trope in *Sherlock* fanfiction).

"Every day I pinch myself that I can have this much fun," Kyndall said to me before she hung up. "Because I've not had fun most of my life."

It's amazing the difference a change in perspective can make.

❤

I WRITE BACK TO VANESSA, THE PROLIFIC FANFICTION author, rephrasing my question now that I've received vicarious therapy. "Would you describe your obsession more like a hobby?" In her reply I recognize that tone I use when my children finally work out an extremely obvious I Spy clue. "Absolutely! That is exactly how I view it." When she started writing her story, she says, she never meant for it to be the magnum opus it's become. She just keeps writing it because it's fun. She finds it really satisfying. "It's like an old friend that is always there for me. I'm very proud of this work," Vanessa says, "and intend to see it through to the end."

That sounds so nice, to be proud of what you love, and to

embrace your feelings about it. How did I end up here instead, scoffing and fearful? I'm writing a book about how I fell in love with Benedict Cumberbatch HAHAHAHAHA, searching for answers as to why such a stupid and embarrassing thing could have happened to me, a perfectly normal person, and what it could all possibly mean. But what if, like Vanessa, I somehow managed to resist the assumption that such a thing requires an explanation? What if I stopped looking at what happened to me and started looking at how it made me feel—afraid, embarrassed, guilty, ashamed—and then asked questions about why. I mean, really, why? Why does something that should feel good feel so bad?

chapter four

this is a chapter
about labels

"How do I fit in?"

I thought this story started with motherhood, but I see now I was wrong. It was high school. Of course it was high school! Everything starts there, always. It's true that Benedict Cumberbatch won't turn up in my life for another twenty years, but that hardly matters. He was already warming up in the wings, because he's a good actor, dedicated to his roles. And I am still thinking about him anyway, because writing this, here and now, Benedict Cumberbatch is all I think about.

Like that time when he was profiled very early in his career, back when he was still ginger, back when he still smoked. The journalist from the *Sunday Times* is distracted by something during the interview. Whenever Benedict Cumberbatch leans forward to ash his cigarette or sip his gin and tonic, she can see the tag sewn into the collar of his white shirt. It reads *Benedict Cumberbatch*. It's a school shirt from his teenage years boarding at Harrow, labeled so it won't get mixed up with the other students' uniforms in the laundry. He's in his late twenties at this point but apparently not old enough (or famous enough) to have left the vestiges of adolescence entirely behind.

"Oh, no. Am I wearing a shirt with a name tag in it?" he says. "My God, and you noticed. I just hadn't done any washing for a while, and this seemed clean. Oh, no—now there will be an article in the *Sunday Times* saying I'm a prat." Like I said—everything *always* starts with high school, even for Benedict Cumberbatch.

I was such a precocious child that high school started for me when I was seven. I wasn't actually *at* high school yet, but I had already worked out everything I needed to know about it. There are many disadvantages to being the youngest child in the family, such as no one bothering to take baby photos of you—when you reach your page in the photo album, it just reads *See above*—but the reward is accelerated learning as you draw from your siblings' one-step-ahead lives. I have two older sisters and an older brother, but it's my two sisters, in particular, who have always offered up instructive examples of what to do and what not to do. Like when my sister Amber wore a purple wig to school.

This occurred on Amber's first-ever high school mufti day, a significant event in any Australian student's life, being the one time when you can cast off your school uniform and turn up to class wearing whatever you like. Believing that the occasion was about freedom of self-expression, Amber got to thinking about her outfit. *I'm fun*, she thought. And what says "fun" better than a giant purple clown's wig? There is literally nothing more fun. Except maybe if you paired it with a matching two-piece, purple fleecy track suit? So she went full Grimace.

When Tamsin, the eldest sister, a small but valuable two years wiser than her, saw what was happening, she immediately burst out the front door to get a head start on the walk to school, keeping as much distance as possible from the human eggplant in her wake.

There was no such need on the way home. Amber had jammed the wig into her backpack, where it and "fun" belonged: behind her.

When Amber had arrived at school, she immediately realized her mistake, of course, and by extension, so had I. Mufti day isn't about freedom of expression; it's about swapping one uniform for another, the ever-changing but meticulously prescribed code of acceptable civvies. This other uniform—which does not typically, nor ever, include a purple wig—is designed to make the hot girls look even hotter, and to ensure that everyone else in their assigned place below them remains invisible. *Who am I?* is not the right question to ask yourself in high school. The right question is *How do I fit in?*

Many years later it would be my turn to go to high school, right after Amber graduated. I knew not to stick my neck out, but some things are impossible to hide. During my first week, sitting quietly in my assigned homeroom, an older boy with an undercut and an untucked shirt asked me, loudly, when I would be getting a nose job. To simply go on having a schnoz like mine was apparently unthinkable. The class sniggered, but I didn't even blush. Everything was going as I expected.

And that was how everything continued to go. I don't mean to give the impression I was picked on. I didn't stick my nose above the parapet long enough for that to even happen. I was of little interest to the loudest voices, who knew my place as well as I did. A few years ago, a boy from school tracked me down so he could apologize for the way he had treated me back then. But I think he had me mixed up with some other nerd, because I don't remember him having anything at all to do with me. I do remember a popular girl called Kelly—blond, shiny, long-limbed—who, while sitting on a bench in the gymnasium during PE class, reached down and brushed her hand up my bare shin, from my ankle sock to my knee. "Prickly," was all she said, wincing. I guess she wanted to see what an uncool girl felt like. It was as she expected.

If not quite so literally, I was, like Kelly, feeling my way through adolescence, working out where I fitted into the social order and what labels I wore. Some girls were goths, some girls played field hockey, other girls loved horses. Tamsin painted David Bowie lyrics above her bed and styled herself as Sally Bowles from *Cabaret* (big noses run in the family). Amber favored the Doors and the Beatles and, for a time, the Sex Pistols, dutifully signing her name with the anarchy symbol. She gave me my first albums, *Achtung Baby* and *Kick*, purchased from the bargain bin at the local record store, and just like that, I embraced my birthright and became a music fan. *These will do nicely*, I must have concluded as I cracked open the cassette cases, since I went ahead and became completely obsessed with both U2 and INXS for years, without any thought of shopping around for other possible objects of infatuation.

I had a lot of feelings and no reason to leave my bedroom—certainly Kelly wasn't inviting me anywhere—so I was ripe for an obsession. I conscientiously collected all of U2's back catalog and sent away my money order to join their official fan club. I soaked up anything of their milieu, which is how, ridiculously, I ended up teaching myself Irish (*Dia duit!*). What I'm saying is, when I get into something, I do it properly. It wasn't quite the same thing with INXS, though. I just really *got into* Michael Hutchence, if you know what I mean. I would cut photos of him into heart shapes and then stickytape them to my skin, where I approximated my own heart to be. I would secretly wear him like that all day, under my school shirt, until the paper had softened to feel like cotton.

I cannot really tell you why I was obsessed with these things, or even if they were worthy of my attention. For many years after my U2 obsession, Amber would successfully torment me by singing the Grandmaster Flash lyrics "Don't push me 'cause I'm close to the edge" in my vicinity, as a reminder of how I once loved something so stupid as a band whose guitarist was called The Edge. But in my teenage bedroom, I truly felt that a man called The Edge was one of the only things worth living for. Tamsin noted with some concern for me at the time that obsessions pursued as deeply as mine were a way to hide from real-world troubles. I remember thinking that this sounded like a reasonable argument, except in my case my obsessions were not a distraction from life but my only actual life source, so there was nothing for anyone to worry about.

At sixteen, I was ready to expand my obsessiveness to cover an entire genre: Britpop. I had worked out by then that it wasn't enough to just be a "music fan"; you had to identify as a particular *kind* of music fan. And I knew, as clear as the nose on my face, that I couldn't be a fangirl or a groupie. To be that kind of fan you had to enter into discussions of ogling—ogling guys in bands and being ogled in return. What else are fangirls for, after all? But since I had been certified "prickly," public ogling was stressful territory for me. Obviously nobody would want *me* to throw my undies at them, and what if I ogled a guy who was out of my league? Rather than inevitably losing this competition, I opted out of it entirely by starting a Britpop fanzine (what can I say—it was the 1990s and I was all in). This would set me apart! It would announce that I wasn't a teenybopper, but a connoisseur. Part of the industry, even.

Tamsin wangled me work experience at a record label so I could discover more about this industry I was supposedly part of. Still precocious, I learned exactly what I needed to know on my first day there. I was crouching on the floor, carrying out my designated task of filing away promotional CDs, when I looked up to see one of the publicists, or "PR girls" as everyone called them, standing on her desk. She was hanging up a huge poster for a new album from Aussie pub rockers the Screaming Jets, with a brooding gorilla on the cover. As she held the poster aloft, her knotted flannel shirt lifted up to show her belly button. The gap between her leather miniskirt and knee-high boots elongated more than seemed even possible. I knew that if I ran my hand along that expanse of leg, it would feel perfectly smooth. I was reminded of *The Raft of the Medusa*, which we had just studied in art class. A pyramid of reaching, exposed flesh. We had learned the story behind the painting too, how the weakest on that raft were eaten by the others. Many threw themselves into the sea in despair.

"How does it look?" she called out across the open-plan office. So I looked. I looked at everyone working there and noticed that apart from the PR girls, they were all men wearing T-shirts over long-sleeve T-shirts. This *Raft of the Sexy Gorilla* situation was apparently the only role available to women here. "It looks great!" I shouted, enthusiastically. I returned to the floor, sorting the CDs into slots, everything in its assigned place. It did not look great. It looked exactly like high school.

Back in my bedroom, writing my fanzine, I worked out how I could be "part of the industry" without having to show my belly button. I decided I would be a music journalist, like all the men whose articles I devoured in the British music press (precisely three months after the publication date, which was how long it took for the magazines to ship to

Australian newsstands). After all, I was practically a journalist already, what with my fanzine. You see, I'm calling it a "fanzine" now, but actually, at the time, I referred to it in my "editorials" as a "publication." I was the best kind of fan—a pro.

I might have been invisible at school, but with my fanzine, I had a *platform*. I faxed interview requests to record labels from my dad's home office and even got replies, which tells you a lot about the authority of a fax machine number. I remember the look on the PR girl's face when I turned up, a sixteen-year-old in men's pants and a T-shirt over a long-sleeve T-shirt, to interview band members from minor Britpop stars Ash—in a pub! I was even invited to the press conference for Anglophile icon Billy Bragg when he toured Sydney, as a member of the actual press! Later, when *Almost Famous* was released, I tried to tell everyone that this was, kind of, once like me, in my mind at least. I was the wunderkind music writer portrayed in that movie, the professional fan and true believer, doing it all for the music, but by then I was nineteen and bore so little resemblance to him that it was hard for anyone to imagine.

Toward the end of my time at high school, a debate was raging in the letters pages of the British music newspaper *NME*, which I was following closely (but three months late) while editing my fanzine. It started with someone calling themselves Ross Towers complaining that Blur concerts were now filled with ten- to thirteen-year-old girls or "knicker-wetters." "Go home and listen to your Take That albums,"

Ross Towers wrote, tossing in a sneering reference to the manufactured boy band whose pop songs dominated the British charts at the time. "Go to your concerts, do what you like, but keep away from Blur and other bands like them." I love the idea that the spectrum of musical seriousness goes from Take That at one end all the way to . . . *Blur* at the other end? What a time it was. Anyway, among the replies to the letter, a fifteen-year-old girl wrote in to defend her right to see whatever bands she wanted, and good on her. Then she went on to say: "The funny part is I hate the girls at the concerts too. But because they're bitchy and ignorant and fickle. Not because they're young."

When I saw this letter on the page, I knew it was all over for me. I immediately recognized the argument she was trying to make, and seeing it spelled out, it looked bad. Very bad. It was the same dubious line I walked with my fan-produced magazine that was definitely not a fanzine. As we said back in the nineties, you can't have your focaccia and eat it too.

Here's another spectrum of seriousness, not of bands, but of fans. At the one end, you have the teenagers, the knicker-wetters, the groupies, and the fangirls. At the other, you have Ross Towers, the credible, authentic man fan. That fifteen-year-old letter writer had the same problem as me. Where did we fit? If we wanted to be seen as serious authorities on music, we were unavoidably aligning ourselves with Ross Towers, even though he obviously despised us because we were, as far as he was concerned, "the girls at the concerts."

And then we had no choice but to hate the girls at the concerts too, because that's how taking sides works. *We* were at one end and *they* were at the other. "We're not like *them!*" we shouted from our music publications. "We're more like . . ." What? Self-hating knicker-wetters?

When you're a girl who really loves a thing, it's never just about you and your thing. Everyone else makes it their problem. You can't love the thing unseen, not even in your bedroom, alone. You either point-blank love the wrong thing (Take That), or you love the right thing (Blur) but in the wrong way (screaming at concerts), or for the wrong reasons (ogling). You can try to sidestep judgment by loving your thing more like a man would (part of the industry!), but sadly you remain a girl, so now you're a fake ("I hate the girls at the concerts too!") and being fake is even worse than loving the wrong thing to begin with. Or at least it was at the time, an era when the guitarist from the Manic Street Preachers carved *4 REAL* into his arm with a razor to demonstrate to a journalist his commitment to the rock-'n'-roll ethic. This was a competition I was born *2 LOSE*. I wasn't hot enough to be a fangirl, not man enough to be legit. "Knowing your place" had turned into a game of musical chairs where, one by one, the seats became unavailable to me despite my frantic semiotic gymnastics. I was a girl wearing men's pants with nowhere to go.

I stopped doing the fanzine. That was easier than acknowledging that all this labeling and sorting of people, myself included, into categories of appropriate behavior based on their superficial attributes was proving to be extremely limiting. That would have required thinking outside the box, and if high school had taught me anything, it was that you stay in your box.

I recognize that my understanding of the social order was not imaginative, or courageous, but I didn't have reason to change tack. All the signals I received about my place in the world simply reinforced that I was right to see myself through the filter of how others saw me. Look, for example, at a book I bought with the money I earned from my fanzine's three-dollar cover price. It is called *Love Is the Drug: Living as a Pop Fan*, and I treated it like a bible. I thumbed its pages over and over, and underlined great passages written by music journalists who got to "live" as "pop fans"! You'll find essays by seventeen journalists in that collection—only two of whom are women. In the introduction, editor John Aizlewood acknowledges this. "I'm sorry there aren't more women writing for this book," he writes, and then offers the following reasons why it might have happened that way. "Firstly, being more mature than men, maybe women reach and discard their obsessions earlier. Secondly, music journalism is a macho thing and, shamefully, women aren't made welcome enough to see it through." He concludes, "Decide for yourself. I genuinely don't know."

I decided for myself. By the end of high school, not only had I given up any last hope of becoming a music journalist, I had stopped being a fan too. Given the choice of eat or be eaten, I threw myself into the sea.

And it was great in there! It was no sacrifice at all. In fact, I was happy to abandon ship. The water was lovely once you were in. I fit right in with all the other girls who had aged out of their interests and discarded their obsessions in the name of maturity, just like that book said we would.

From that point on, I liked indie bands and art-house films, but not any particular one more than the others. I pursued pastimes like hipster crafts and shopping for home-wares and studying French, in a restrained but still very enjoyable way. After so long trying, and failing, to contort my feelings into socially acceptable shapes, it was a relief to abandon them for pleasures that required no justification and attracted no finger-pointing. Women don't "see it through," the book said, and why would we? If we carted our juvenile obsessions into adulthood (weird!), we wouldn't be able to enjoy that satisfying feeling of everything slotting into its right place.

And anyway, teenagers seemed so lame to me now, especially the teenage me. Adolescence had just been a chrysalis, an intermediary stage in my life cycle, from which I emerged as the finished product, a grown-up. The version of me who drew The Edge in Artline pen in my visual diary or wanted to spend the rest of my life writing music reviews was not fully formed. She got me to where I needed to be, and once her purpose was served, I was done with her. Except to deploy her as comic fodder, of course, because it's so easy to joke about teenage girls. They're larvae! One day soon they'll grow up and join us in laughing at themselves too, because the jokes are not really at their expense but the phase they're in. *Britpop, LOL!* They'll find their old fanzine and read out the most cringeworthy bits for us and we can all hoot along, safe in the knowledge that we have ascended.

♥

LOOKING BACK AT MY TEENAGE MANIAS, I HAVE ALWAYS been grateful for how they got me through some of the most difficult years of my life, and also for helping me win many trivia rounds on nineties music. But I have never missed them. Not once since then did I sit back and say to myself, *What I really want right now is to completely and utterly lose myself in an obsession with such intensity that I will be inspired to take up Irish.* I did not touch my skin and feel the absence of a paper heart.

It would be easy, now, for me to draw for you the direct, unsurprising line carrying me from Michael Hutchence to Benedict Cumberbatch. All aboard for lithe, sensitive performers with great hair! Next stop: Harry Styles! But that's not what my journey looked like. I did not follow a route determined by the things I loved; the things I loved were determined by the route, my graduation from one life stage to the next. Which is why falling in love with Benedict Cumberbatch didn't feel natural or unsurprising at all. It felt like a step backward, in the very wrong direction. I had been through all this before, and that was exactly the problem.

I experienced an actual Proustian moment in Gymboree class (classic Proust), while sitting on the floor among a circle of toddlers clapping their sticky little hands together and the other moms, all of us wearing socks and expressions of forbearance. I had my phone discreetly in my lap and was idly tracing the shape of Benedict Cumberbatch's luminous cheekbone on the lock screen. And then I suddenly, and vividly, remembered running those same fingers along the seam of Michael Hutchence's open shirt, as it appeared on the cover of *The Face* magazine in 1991. It wasn't a comforting memory; it was terrifying.

As soon as I got home from Gymboree, I changed the photo on my phone. When you're a mother, the photo on your phone is supposed to be of your kids.

chapter five

this is a chapter about guilt

"Yeah, kids are great, but have you seen Benedict Cumberbatch?"

After many hours in labor, the reason my son was born via cesarean was, according to my medical record, "failure to progress." What a boon, to be given both a baby *and* a metaphor for my life as a mother— on the same day! I was a bit disappointed not to receive any fresh material when, around two years later, the cesarean birth of my daughter was also, boringly, attributed to my "failure to progress." But I had to accept that the doctors were right: the failure to progress hadn't ended since the first birth. This was not a brand-new failure but a continuation of the last ongoing one.

A part of me thinks I got pregnant the second time just to legitimize the fact that I was still wearing maternity pants from the first. It also meant I didn't have to feel bad about failing to progress my "home yoga practice" beyond the introductory postpartum routine, designed for when your baby is six weeks old and you're ready to "get back on the mat." I was still doing that class when my son was taking his own yoga classes at preschool. The athleisure-clad yoga teacher on my laptop would tell me how proud she was of me for making this time for myself while I completed a routine that was basically just lying on the floor. I hardly ever did it anyway.

As I failed to progress, on and on, never getting anywhere with anything, my ambitions for what I could achieve contracted around me, like the opposite of a koi carp growing to the size of its pond. I am reminded of when my friend Kate, who has kids around the same age as mine, told me she was going to volunteer to be treasurer of her playgroup, which seemed extremely out of character. Kate is a wonderful musician who used to tour for weeks at a time all over Australia, but she had been unable to write songs since becoming a mother. Every time she tried to compose something, she told me, she would realize she had nicked the tune from *Big Block SingSong*. Whenever she tried to play the guitar, her shoulder would pulse with pain caused by hauling and holding babies. Being playgroup treasurer, she believed, was at least one way she felt she could spread her wings, and make progress, in other areas of her life. The next time I heard from Kate, she reported, "I am involved in sifting cat poo out of the playgroup sandpit and replacing the sand!" It's an awkward position from which to spread your wings.

I found myself in the same position when, after years getting by on freelance work, I got a job on a university science communications team. This, I thought, was my opportunity to finally get somewhere, to expand beyond my confines! But my failure to progress only . . . progressed. On my first day, I dressed in whatever ragtag combination of clothes would fit my new shape—a long-sleeved top and leggings under a gaping summer dress, with some random unbuttoned shirt on top of it all—making me look like Helena Bonham Carter but not good. I took a knife to the crusty lid of my bottle of foundation to prize it open and feverishly whisked the wand of my mascara to bring it back to life. I looked in the mirror and admired my creation, the professional woman. I put baby Dulcie into our bicycle trailer and dragged her behind me to day care, sweating off my makeup as I pedaled. Once she'd been deposited there, I unhitched the trailer in the parking lot of the day care center and sped off to my work on my bicycle, unhindered. Nothing would weigh me down! Nothing would hold me back!

But at work I was so tired from all the night-wakings that I was hallucinating the computer keys floating above the keyboard. Now I was Helena Bonham Carter in a Tim Burton film, but still not good. An email came through from the day care center about a stomach flu outbreak, and I forwarded it to Nathan so we could argue at home later about who would take the parental leave when the time inevitably came. My colleagues talked about staying late to take photos at a university awards night, while I had to launch myself out of the door for day care collection time, literally midway through typing a sentence. It was probably a bad sentence anyway, because of the floating keys. And on it went the next day, and the next, with the overall effect of Sisyphus and the rolling rock, or maybe Kate and the sifting sand.

My manager, out of consideration, didn't pressure me to attend after-hours events, so I didn't go, and I didn't make the important networking connections that happen there. The cost of child care meant it only made financial sense for me to work part time, which also meant I could never be considered for a promotion, which were all for full-time roles. My junior colleagues would soon leapfrog me. On Wednesdays, the end of my working week, they would say, "Enjoy your days off!" And then because they're considerate people who know that it's hard to be a working mother, they'd correct themselves to say, "No, your days at work are your real days off, aren't they!" But it's not a question of which days to refer to, it's a matter of there never being an "off." Unlike a bicycle trailer, it turns out you can't conveniently unhitch motherhood from who you are.

I'm sure you knew that already. None of this is breaking news; it was just new to me. And I'm sure you also know that none of this ranks as even slightly bad on the scale of parenting experiences. In fact, it's all the way up the other end of the scale, where the best possible experiences occur. Plus, having parented through a pandemic now, I know the advantages of having an office to go to. Imagine complaining about that! Compared to homeschooling while working from home, the mere option of being able to go *somewhere else* is a luxury. But it would be historical revisionism to say my office was ever truly a sanctified child-free zone, because even back then, there was nothing in my life that wasn't at least partially subsumed into motherhood. I just got to be a mother in multiple physical locations.

This makes me think of a vintage brooch I once saw in an antique jewelry store. It had gold cursive script spelling out *Mother*, with delicate little pearls inside the lettering and a big swoosh beneath to underline the word. I pictured the Mother who once owned it, smiling at herself in the dressing-table mirror as she pinned it on, this very beautiful label. I found it strange that she would want to announce herself in this way, because when you are a mother, being Mother is already so close to the surface of everything you do that adding extra decorative layers hardly seems necessary. But perhaps she deployed the brooch like a kind of taxi light. If the brooch is on, the Mother is available. And then, thrillingly, the brooch can come off! There she is, stretched on a chaise longue, a novel in one hand, a martini in the other; when someone approaches her with questions regarding the whereabouts of their karate uniform, she points to her bare lapel, smiles, and shakes her head. No, the Mother is not available.

Embarrassingly, I think that before I had kids, this is what I believed motherhood would be like, something you could toggle on and off as it suited you. Also I thought you could read novels. But the reality is, mere days into parenthood, I had already joined several Facebook mothers' groups where members referred to one another as "Mama" as if that were all we were. Those groups were actually really useful, because we were all mamas now.

There is—and isn't this always the case?—a headline from the *Onion* that illustrates this perfectly: "Mom Hasn't Ordered Favorite Pizza Topping in over a Decade." It's funny 'cause it's true. The story opens, *Saying that "it's fine, really," local mother Catherine Reynolds told reporters Wednesday that she has not been able to order her favorite pizza topping, spinach, in nearly 12 years.* That's the joke of motherhood: you don't get to have children *and* be yourself. When you eat pizza, you eat pizza *as a mother.* Every day—hundreds of times a day, every day—you give up what you want and how you want it in so many tiny little ways, that whatever squeezed-out orange-half remains of you, that's who you are now. It's fine, really.

I had seen this happen to other women, of course, but I thought they were at best unlucky and at worst conventional. In my mind, I had a number of escape routes to divert me from their doomed path: large, smug exit signs labeled *Evolved Husband* and *Flexible Workplace* and *Gender Equality.* But once I gave birth, I was shocked at how unstoppable and how inevitable the sequence of events became, as I too was propelled down the road called "The Way Things Are," and one by one, the turnoffs to my planned exit routes disappeared over my shoulder.

Soon after I started the university job, I interviewed a quantitative mental health researcher, Dr. Liana Leach, for a story about parenting trends. We talked about our own parenting too, how we split the care of our children with our partners, and how we balanced home life with work. At the time, she was conducting surveys of parents, and she told me that in the process of sorting results, her eyes would land on the survey question that asked participants, "How often do you feel rushed or pushed for time? Always. Often. Sometimes. Never." She would silently mouth her own answer: Always. She repeats it: *Always*. If it's not rushing at work, it's rushing to get things done at home. It's an intensified way of being, all the time, where you feel like there's no space."

Dr. Leach was using Facebook ads to recruit parents to her survey. But looking at the responses coming in, she noticed that although she was targeting both men and women, 98 percent of her respondents were mothers. "When we realized what was happening," she says, "we ran a second set of advertisements." The only change they made to the ad was in the wording: the word "parents" was changed to "dads." Only then did men start replying, because they didn't think the first ad, for parents, was meant for them. Because to them, "parenting" is actually just "mothering."

The fathers couldn't see themselves as parents, and I, the Mother, couldn't see myself as anything else. The parenting, the mothering, went all the way to the edges of me, and even slightly beyond the edges too, like coloring-in that didn't stay between the lines. There was no space for anything else, as Dr. Leach said. Fathers are able to see themselves as other things because, typically, their professional identity is less affected by having children, and also because they simply have the uninterrupted time and the space to do so—thanks to mothers doing more than their share of unpaid care and domestic work. In the United States, fathers get almost twice as much child-free leisure time as mothers; in the UK, men get over an hour of extra leisure time every day. A 2018 study found that one in three Australian women do not, on a weekly basis, get time to themselves *at all*.

I type that and I can hear Lea in my mind right now, saying, "Tabitha, it only gets worse!" And that reminds me, this isn't just about motherhood.

❤

LEA IS SEVENTY YEARS OLD AND BEGINS A LOT OF HER sentences with "When you get to my age . . ." We met on Twitter after I was carrying on about how motherhood sucks up your identity and she replied, "Maybe some day I'll write from the perspective of a 'senior citizen.'" This was her polite, introductory version of "When you get to my age . . ." Which itself is a polite version of "You don't even know what you're talking about, young lady." And, I mean, she's not wrong. There are still many things at play here that I don't understand. I tell Lea she doesn't need to wait until "some day" to get on her soapbox, and I give her a call to hear her perspective.

Lea lives in Ohio—just like Kyndall, from earlier. They don't know each other, though. Why would they? They just both live in Ohio. And yet I have no explanation for why I, here in Canberra, am making these random connections with total strangers on the internet and they all end up being from Ohio, a place I've never been. But so far I really like everyone who lives there.

Lea's patch of Ohio is fifty acres of woods, surrounded by state forest, located somewhere between a small town and a smaller town. When I call her up, I ask what animals live on her property and she says, "Just your raccoons and squirrels and normal woodsy critters." I tell her that even squirrels are exciting to Australians, and then regale her with a story about the inundation of kangaroos in our "Bush Capital"—a real thing that was happening at the time. She listens patiently, then says, "I don't know any of your animals in Australia."

She's lived on her property for thirty years, with her husband and a changing cast of Jack Russells. Her son lives next door. It's hard living. If they have three feet of snow, or if it floods, they have to bail themselves out. When you live in the city, you're set up to be rescued; in the country, you're the victim and the rescuer. It's a "redneck area," she says. "There's no sophistication here at all. The men are all about hunting, and riding four-wheelers through the woods, and being real macho, and drinking, and fishing, and doing all the traditional manly things. The women . . ." She trails off. "Well, they're not going anywhere with me when I ask them to. They're at home, doing domestic things."

Lea wouldn't say she's unhappy with her life, particularly when she compares it to those of the women around her. "The thing is, I'm with women all day," she says. She runs a nail salon in town, where she says her job "is to sit across a table from a woman and hold their hand for anywhere between thirty minutes to an hour and a half." They tell her everything. Most of Lea's clients are between forty and ninety years old, and if they're not looking after their husbands or aging parents, they're looking after their grandchildren on behalf of their daughters, many of whom have developed drug problems. For a lot of her clients, the only thing they do for themselves *at all* is get their nails done or get a pedicure, because they give everything else to everyone else.

Hearing these cautionary tales day after day, Lea tries to nurture her interests and carve out more time for herself. When she was seventeen, she was in a Paul McCartney fan club that met up every week to trade pictures and talk about the Beatles. That was from 1965 to 1967. Since then there hasn't been much space to develop other interests. She's always been into theater, though. Not performing herself, but the whole world of it, the costumes, the sets. She made friends with people on Tripadvisor and organized to meet them in Las Vegas for shows a few times. I didn't know you could make friends on Tripadvisor, but it was a necessity, she says, since many of her real-life friends hadn't ever left the county. Not the country—the *county*. She loves the trips and the shows, but they're not enough. She wouldn't say she's unhappy with her life, but she's not happy either.

"I tried to make things more like I wanted to be, but I was frustrated," she says. "Things weren't going the way I anticipated or pictured them going. I was just moseying along, coming home from work, fighting with my husband, throwing the ball to the dog. I'm not really old, but at this point it would be hard to start something over again. I love my husband and he loves me, but over the years he's been more self-centered, doing what he wants to do, and I'm more of a compromiser. So at that time, I was just thinking, 'I'm going to wait until this is over.'

"I thought, 'Well, I've had a full life and done a lot of really cool things. I own my property, I own my business, and I love it. I'm not that successful monetarily, but I get to take trips sometimes. Everything is going fine. I shouldn't be complaining.'

"When you get to my age, you've reached a point in your life where there's a hole," she says. "There's something missing. You kind of stop being a woman, like an individual woman, and you start being a mother or a grandma or a wife or an elderly lady. The focus changes from being on yourself. You have to split the focus between kids and husbands and bosses and parents, and then, who are you? I thought, 'Well, that's how it is.'"

I tell her I think I understand what she means and she instantly hits back with "Tabitha, it only gets worse!"

❤

I FELL FOR BENEDICT CUMBERBATCH *AS A MOTHER*. There was no other way for it to be. If there had been a Facebook group called Cumbermamalovers I would have joined it. There is nothing wrong with being a mother, or a mama, of course. Do I have to say that? I love my kids! You would too if you met them, because they are the absolute greatest kids. Truly, they're the best thing that ever happened to me. I would not swap them for anything, not even spinach on my pizza. And I do not want to appear ungrateful! I am so grateful. I have had all the luck and all the advantages the world can throw at a person.

But this is exactly why it felt so wrong to fall for Benedict Cumberbatch *as a mother*. Because what could it mean except that I was dissatisfied with my perfectly good life, and worse, with my healthy, happy family? What I had was not enough and I wanted more, even though, as Lea says, that's just how it is. How terrible! And greedy! And because being a mother went all the way to the edges of me, if I wanted to scrape out a little bit of time or space for anything else, it was at the expense of the motherness. There was no room to add anything else, so it had to be a taking away. So even though I just said, right now, I wouldn't swap my children for anything, I was, unavoidably, swapping motherhood for Benedict Cumberbatch. How is that okay?

I mean, riddle me this: When something as objectively meaningful as motherhood left me feeling unfulfilled, why did I turn instead to something as gobsmackingly unimportant (no offense) as Benedict Cumberbatch? Of all things, why was that the trade I made? I had no time and space to progress anything of any substance in my life, and now, all of a sudden, I've made eight hours available to listen to Benedict Cumberbatch doing the voice of Rumpole of the Bailey on audiobook? Of course it felt wrong; it felt like being a bad mother. That is what it feels like to want more.

In an essay that appears in a book called *On Being 40(ish)*, the writer Taffy Brodesser-Akner says the essential conundrum of middle age comes down to this: "How can you be this dissatisfied when you have this much? How can you be this satisfied when you have so little?" Brodesser-Akner writes that it's okay not to have any answers, but in my mind, I turn these questions over again and again.

I'm doing the same thing with the words "obsession" and "hobby." I'm now trying to avoid labeling what happened to me as an obsession, but surely it's not exactly a hobby either? When I think of hobbies, I immediately get an image of this book on ikebana—the Japanese art of flower arranging—that my mother owned in the 1980s. I don't recall my mother actually doing any ikebana, but if she did, would it have made her feel bad? And has ikebana ever given anyone cause to see a psychologist? Perhaps. Let's not rule anything out.

"Invisible leisure" is a term I learned from Brigid Schulte in her book about time pressure, *Overwhelmed*. This is what she calls the productive, socially sanctioned activities like quilting bees, canning parties, knitting circles, and book groups, which are, she says, truly "the only kind of acceptable and industrious leisure time most women have ever known." Invisible leisure is typically task-oriented, often domestic, and "purposive," she says, directed to meeting the needs of family, friends, and community. You might look like you're having fun—you could even be on holiday!—but you're still on call. There's a perfect headline from the *Onion* for this too: "Mom Spends Beach Vacation Assuming All Household Duties in Closer Proximity to Ocean." This is why the true test of leisure, Schulte says, is not *what* activity you're doing but how that time *feels*. Did that beach trip really feel like a holiday?

When it happens, *pure* leisure should feel like play, not work. You won't be worrying about whether everyone else is having a good time; you won't be lumped with the labor—physical, mental, or emotional—of planning, delegating, and cleaning up; you won't be doing it out of obligation, because you know it's good for you. Pure leisure requires a deliberate choice to carve out nonpurposive time just for yourself. For women, Schulte explains, that's "nothing less than a courageous—subversive, almost—act of resistance." But shouldn't that feel good?

❤

THERE IS A NAIL SALON, SOMEWHERE IN OHIO, COVERED in pictures of Benedict Cumberbatch.

Does it matter how it really started? ("I was flipping through some channels trying to find something to watch.") Or what happened next? ("Benedict came on and I thought, 'Egads, he's weird! He really looks odd.' Then I fell in love with the guy.") Or even why? ("It's his focus, the energy that he puts out. And his vocabulary.") Just know that Lea worked out that it *didn't* have to be this way. If there's something missing, if there's a hole in your life, you can fill it. It turns out that for Lea, the hole happened to be shaped exactly like Benedict Cumberbatch.

"I realized I had talked myself into believing that this is just how it is. But then Benedict came along and I remembered that it doesn't have to be. He woke me up. He filled up my imagination. It sounds dorky, but he changed my life around. He got me on a track of not feeling sorry for myself anymore. It started as small things, but then I went to London because of him! I'd never been out of the country, so it was sort of a big deal. But it was the best thing I ever did."

Lea tells me how she saw Benedict Cumberbatch as Hamlet at the Barbican in London, twice ("Electrifying!"), and met him at the stage door afterward ("And there he was!"), briefly. I've never been so close to Benedict Cumberbatch, so I ask a lot of questions. She tells me that standing face-to-face with him, she felt the urge to reach out and touch his cheek. "I said to myself, 'No, don't even think about doing that!' but his cheek was right in front of my eye and it looked so soft." She felt guilty about that, looking at him that way (oh, this is a whole other world of guilt we'll have to get to later), but then they made eye contact and she said thank you. "For being him," she says. "For entertaining me." Later, Lea travels to Los Angeles for a *Sherlock* convention. She meets Benedict Cumberbatch's mother, the actress Wanda Ventham, and gives her a professional-quality nail file as a gift. Wanda is delighted and puts it straight into her handbag. Lea says that was to say thank you too, for making Benedict Cumberbatch.

Back at the nail salon, Lea's clientele don't really know who he is, this Benedict Cumberbatch. "They don't watch PBS. They wouldn't even know what the BBC is. But they know I love Benedict and so they buy me things." The photos on the walls started when one of her clients gave her a Benedict Cumberbatch calendar. "I was like, 'Where am I going to put this?' And the person who was there in the salon was like, 'Put it up! I want to see it.'"

Now the photos serve as a reminder, she says, to her, but mostly to her clients. "You should allow yourself more than a nail appointment. You should indulge in things that refresh your spirit or make you laugh or make you feel something." She sighs. "People deserve indulgences. I wish they could do more. I tell them, 'Go somewhere! Do something! Feel something! Anything!'"

I remember my colleague who looked at my desk covered in Benedict Cumberbatch photos and thought it was ironic. There's something kitschy too in the image of elderly women in a rural nail salon that's papered with pinups of the Sexiest Man Alive (confirmed by numerous polls). But I listen to Lea and I think, *There's no way anyone could mistake that for irony.* It sounds more like radical and subversive resistance.

I ask Lea if she ever feels guilty about how she uses her time. "At first, I felt silly, because of my age," she says. "I thought, 'You shouldn't be doing this: falling in love with this young guy, looking at pictures, collecting DVDs, and reading all this stuff. You shouldn't be spending all this time on something so juvenile at your age. That's more for younger women.' That's what I thought. It was only when I came across other people who were not afraid to share their feelings and they turned out to be just like mine—which was a surprise—then I didn't feel like it was inappropriate. All of a sudden, I was seeing all these other women in their late sixties and early seventies who feel the same way. We're all thinking and feeling the exact same thing."

Now, she doesn't feel guilty at all. "You know, there are a lot of people, their lives revolve around golf. They don't feel guilty."

❤

PEOPLE SOMETIMES ASK ME IF I THINK BENEDICT Cumberbatch will read this book. I tell them, "Thankfully, no, he's a very busy man." But when my kids, Teddy and Dulcie, ask me if they can read it someday, I say, "Yes, of course!" with a smile that is really a panicked grimace because this prospect is much more terrifying than the Benedict Cumberbatch one. They can read now. Isn't that amazing? I still remember when Teddy first worked out how to open the car door and climb inside by himself. I was so overcome with excitement at how many seconds—maybe even a whole minute!—this would save me per day that we went out for ice cream to celebrate. Then there was the day he said he was thirsty and went off to fill his own cup of water from the tap, and I almost started sobbing with relief. Now he can read. And I'm on, like, level two of my home yoga class. I get to go on work trips. Sometimes I read novels. It's hard to explain how it happened, how the ratio eventually became slightly more progress than failure, but it feels like the car door and the tap thing were important.

And now one day my kids will read this book, and when they finish this chapter—which could be subheaded *Yeah, kids are great, but have you seen Benedict Cumberbatch?*—they'll slam it down on the kitchen counter and say, "Let me ask you, what kind of mother would write a book like this?" And I'll shout frantically: "The Mother is not available!" So they'll climb up on a stool to look me right in the eyes and say, "Answer us, dammit!" And I'll say, "Shhh, keep it down," because I don't want Nathan to hear. That's another conversation I'm trying to avoid, the one about this book and what-kind-of-wife.

The truth is, I don't know what-kind-of-mother. I can't get a clear image of her, what label she wears: Distracted Mother? Ungrateful Mother? Resentful Mother? Guilty Mother? That's a lot of gold, a lot of little pearls. What about your mother? Would she have written a book like this? Did she have *pure* leisure in her life, something that was just for herself, something that wasted her time? Did she have the space? And would that have made her feel good?

chapter six

this is a chapter about hiding

"I don't want anyone to know about any of this."

I don't know if you've ever discovered a note hidden in a library book, but in my opinion, it's one of the most exciting things that can happen to a person. Even if it's an old shopping list being used as a bookmark, you now have a connection to another human being who once held the same book in their hands and read the same words as you. A total stranger is now one step closer to being someone Just Like Me.

When the kids were smaller, we used to go to the library almost every day. My library has two different biographies of Benedict Cumberbatch; the Patrick Melrose and the *Parade's End* novels with Benedict Cumberbatch on the cover; and a coffee table book about *Sherlock* with behind-the-scenes photos and production information. The library also has other books, without Benedict Cumberbatch in them, and once a week, they hold a Giggle and Wiggle song and story time session for kids.

During one such visit, I stepped away from the giggling, wiggling children to take a look on the sly at this *Sherlock* coffee table book. It's a real beauty, featuring many examples of my favorite kind of Benedict Cumberbatch photo, where he's dressed in character but he's not acting; he's waiting around between scenes with a cup of coffee or getting his hair done. I love these pictures because he's two people at once, his real self and his pretend one, and therefore twice as attractive. When I slid the book from the shelf, it fell open in my hands to a double-page photo of Benedict Cumberbatch as Sherlock Holmes, scarf flying as he jumps off the roof of Barts Hospital.

And there, stuck to the page, was a yellow Post-it note. My eyes widened. On the note, there was a URL written in black ink and an invitation: "Come and discuss *Sherlock* with us! (Also great for pictures of Benedict.)" Upping the ante of Giggle and Wiggle, I guffawed and practically fell over.

I looked up from the book and studied the people around me. There was an old man reading a Chinese newspaper through a magnifying glass, a teenage girl sitting cross-legged at a desk charging her phone, a bunch of better mothers than me, doing the actions to "Itsy Bitsy Spider"—any one of them could have left this note. Any one of them could be Just Like Me, here, in *Canberra*! I snapped the book shut and added it to the pile we were borrowing, which was probably mostly picture books about diggers. The rest of Giggle and Wiggle dragged even longer than usual.

At home, I put the library books on the kitchen bench and occupied the children with play dough—"Make as much mess as you want!"—and then typed the website address into my computer, the first step to working out who left the note. It led to an old-school forum, the kind of thing I didn't know still existed in the age of social media, drawing in fans from around the world. As promised, they were sharing photos they had found and discussing the minutiae of *Sherlock* and the rest of Benedict Cumberbatch's body of work. And body. There was a section of the forum where you could introduce yourself. There are *Sherlock* fans of all gender identities—this is a show that at one point was, globally, the most-watched show on Netflix—but on this forum I could only see fans identifying themselves as women. Many contributors said they had been driven there because either no one in their real life understood their obsession or they didn't want to tell anyone else about it. There were a lot of women over thirty, a lot of women over fifty, even. One woman said she had recently worn her *Sherlock* T-shirt to an event she'd attended, hoping that it would spark conversation, but "no one said anything."

To say they seemed one-dimensional is a generous number of dimensions. The whole thing made me squirm. The forum's early-2000s internet aesthetic of blindingly colored fonts on unreadable backgrounds wasn't helping. It was unseemly, the way these people were letting it all hang out. There was a thread where they shared dreams they'd had about him (you could say "him" in this forum with no further explanation necessary), opening up even their subconscious for display. It seemed like the kind of place where people had given up entirely on curating or filtering themselves—the kind of place you went when you had nowhere else to go.

I tried to imagine launching myself into the discussion, declaring I'd found the note, and waving it around to claim my prize, its author. But all I could think of was those enormous, overstuffed animals you see dangling at the games at the county fair, less an incentive to play than a risk of winning. Do you really want to go home with one of those? What kind of person tries to communicate via a secret note hidden in a library book anyway?

Maybe the women on the forum felt like they were hiding in the darkness of the internet, but even here, they already looked overexposed to me. *They should know better*, I thought. They should know how terrible it looks, how unflattering, when you shine a light on your inner workings. Some things are meant to stay hidden. I closed the laptop and felt more alone than before. I sat down with the kids and sculpted Benedict Cumberbatch's weird head out of blue play dough, rubbing my palms together to roll out strands for his curls.

♥

WHEN MY FRIENDS ALL STARTED TURNING FORTY, IT was like they were now able to see a special Bat-Signal calling them to attend something called No Lights No Lycra. In the space of a few months, I went from never having heard, nor quite comprehending, those words in that order to fending off multiple text-message conversations from one friend after another, all over Australia, about their life-changing experiences there. *Yes! Yes! I know all about it!* I replied so many times that eventually I had to attend one myself so this could actually be true.

It is, quite simply, a sixty-minute dance session set to an eclectic soundtrack, held in church or community halls, and open to everyone for a small fee. What's notable about it is it happens in complete darkness. There are no lights and there is no dress code (the "Lycra" in the name refers to the leotards and dance wear required at formal dance classes). There's also no drinking, no chatting, and no hanging around without participating. Everyone is spaced out so there's no risk of bumping into anyone. You have no choice but to dance like nobody's watching.

This is why my friends love it. They tell me they've never felt so liberated, so uninhibited. It's like dancing in your bedroom when you were a teenager, one tells me. "Like therapy and church in one," my best friend says. She then goes on to describe how—to the soundtrack of Salt-N-Pepa's "Push It"—she busted out a dance move so vigorous that it generated enough momentum for her postpregnancy belly to start gyrating to its own rhythm. She is delighted. After I went, I got what she was saying. You should go too. It's a thing that was started in Melbourne by two dancers, Alice Glenn and Heidi Barrett, but it has now spread all around the world.

In an Anglican church hall in Canberra, with "Don't Leave Me This Way" blasting over a pretty average sound system, I did actual high kicks. The song would go, oooooOOOH *baby*! and I would do a high kick right at that bit. I didn't know I could do high kicks. Then they announced that the next song would be the last, and it was "Freedom! '90" by George Michael and I waved my arms around in the air with the titular freedom, until the very second the lights came on. Then I grabbed my water bottle and scuttled out of there, sweaty and red-faced, my head down to avoid eye contact with the other forty-year-old women in the church parking lot, and drove home.

After my visit, I also start to evangelize No Lights No Lycra to other forty-year-old women. They're always interested but want clarification on an important point, about exactly how dark it is in there. They want to know if the curtains are heavy enough to block out the streetlights, or if the glow of the emergency exit sign gives away your outline. I tell them it's extremely dark. Do you think I'm doing high kicks if people can see me? Some things are meant to stay hidden. One friend says she'd like to go, but she'll wait until winter, when she can be sure it will be pitch-black.

I should probably mention that I know—now—what kind of person communicates via hidden notes in a library book. It's the same kind of person who dances in the dark: a person who doesn't want to be seen. A person Just Like Me. But that's the thing about dancing in the dark. It's good that no one can see you, but you can't see each other either. You can't see what good company you're in. All these people, hiding. Just Like You.

❤

IT DOES SEEM THAT IF YOU THROW A DART AT OHIO, you'll hit someone who's in love with Benedict Cumberbatch, doesn't it? "They're called *Cumberbitches*!" screams every single journalist who has ever written about Benedict Cumberbatch, as if this has been uncovered, exclusively, by their deep reporting. Who can blame them? It's a very funny name, immortalized in 2010 by the @Cumberbitches Twitter account along with their manifesto: "Throw your boobs in the air if you want some cumberlovin."

(However, the name *is* controversial, with Benedict Cumberbatch himself worrying that it has "set feminism back so many notches." It does put him in a bit of a pickle. It's a term that holds the power of a reclaimed pejorative only when someone chooses to apply it to themself. So even if his fans want to call themselves Cumberbitches, he can't call them that, which is awkward since journalists ask him about it constantly. Over the past decade, fans have attempted to establish alternative, more inclusive—less funny—monikers like Cumbercollective, Cumberpeople, Cumbercookies, Cumbercommunity, Cumberbunnies, Cumberbabes, and Benaddicts, but none have had the staying power of Cumberbitches. I like the term, and I don't find it offensive, which is why I'm going to keep using it. I apologize in advance if you don't feel this way. I also apologize to feminism, but I think it will be okay.)

If you have fallen in love with Benedict Cumberbatch, or

maybe even if you haven't, then you know about these Cumberbitches, his "rabid female fan base." I certainly knew about them from my earliest googles of Benedict Cumberbatch, back when I still had to think about how to spell his name. You hear them whooping from the audience on his TV talk show appearances. You see them pressing against one another to get an autograph or a selfie as he walks the red carpet, shouting, "We love you, Ben!" (*Ben!*) and making noises as if they actually do have rabies.

You might think that when I found out about the Cumberbitches I was relieved, or thrilled even, to connect with like minds. But no, the Cumberbitches did not make me feel less weird and alone in my ardor for Benedict Cumberbatch; they only made me feel worse. Their very existence was anxiety-inducing, a warning sign. Sure, my whole identity was falling apart as I was unable to work out who I was or what was happening to me, but there was one thing I was certain of: *I* was not *them*.

Remember the guy complaining in the *NME* about girls attending Blur concerts for all the wrong reasons? Fast-forward several decades to a Benedict Cumberbatch profile in the *Times Magazine*, promoting the premiere of *Star Trek Into Darkness*. In the profile, we meet a serious *Star Trek* fan who is waiting on the red carpet, amid a sea of Cumberbitches: "'These people aren't here for *Star Trek*,' she says, casting a hateful eye over the gleefully calling fans. 'They don't even know what *Star Trek* is. They're just here for him.' She jerks a disgusted thumb at Cumberbatch."

I did not want to be disdained by—of all people!—a Trekkie. I did not want to be the subject of a disgusted thumb. Twenty-five years ago, I did not want to be one of the "girls at the concerts"; and now, a grown-ass woman, I really did not want to be a Cumberbitch. Who would? The Cumberbitches were the public face of my private fears. They were the living, whooping proof of how embarrassing and immature it is to be in love with a celebrity. I mean, just look at them! At least I had enough self-loathing—no, sorry, I mean self-respect—to hide my feelings, and to maintain the illusion of being a normal person. That's what made me different.

❤

WHEN A GROUP OF WOMEN OR GIRLS LOVES SOMETHING, it's like the more there are of them, the stupider and more embarrassing their feelings become. You could plot it on a graph. If one woman in love with Benedict Cumberbatch looks ironic, how many women does it take before it starts to look moronic? Like, three? Four? At what point do you change from being a person into a Cumberbitch?

I don't know which example to use to illustrate this. Which mostly feminine group wins the prize for being, en masse, the most easily dismissed? The Lisztomaniacs, the Beatlemaniacs, the Twi-Moms, the Pinterest Moms, the Beliebers, the Directioners, the *Outlander*-ers, the BTS ARMY, romance writers, *Fifty Shades of Grey* readers, *Eat Pray Love* devotees, reality TV watchers, pink-wearing preschoolers, the Cumberbitches? Despite their enormous market power, they devalue the cool factor of everything they touch.

Girl fans of boy bands cop it the worst. They are "bad and wrong," the music critic Anwen Crawford writes, because it's assumed "they don't know how to listen." Instead: "They lust. They look, and the gaze of innumerable girls upon the pretty faces of their boy band idols is a kind of embarrassment, both to the idol and to the world." She then notes, "See how I used the word *pretty* there, without even thinking why—the male musician is made girly by girls. And who would want to be made into a girl, if you don't already have to be one?" Just ask Blur! Not long after that comment about the "girls at the concerts" was published, they abandoned their emasculating pop stylings in favor of a more "sophisticated" sound and image. Blur's bassist Alex James later described this decision to distance themselves from their teen girl fanbase as "a fucking big balls move."

When lots of women love a thing, that's all we need to know about it. And the women too. It translates immediately into an image, plucked from a readily accessible catalog: squealing girls drowning out the band on stage; home-manicured housewives glued to their romance ebooks on their Kindles; that photoshoot Benedict Cumberbatch did for the *New York* magazine story titled "Benedict and the Cumberbitches." In one photo he's slumped, wearily, inside a limo as girls press themselves against the windows. In another, he's in motion, running away from the same girls, their arms stretched out toward him like zombies. Do you reckon I looked at those photos and thought, proudly, *Ahh yes, they're Just Like Me?*

Ever since adolescence, I have known to give a wide berth to these groups of girls and women experiencing *feelings*, otherwise they'll suck you in like a whirlpool. They'll grab you with their zombie arms, and you'll become one of them, trapped like a Beatlemaniac, frozen in time and in black and white, your mouth permanently contorted, your hands clutching your face, forever.

It can start innocently enough, with the simple pursuit of a good feeling, which is why you need to always be on guard. If something feels good, or worse, *too* good, other girls will want to come along for the ride, then together, you'll inevitably end up somewhere bad. "An ocean of 20,000 wide-opening mouths, hundreds of pleading white eyes, 40,000 palms raised skywards" is the image that *GQ* supplies for a One Direction concert. A "dark-pink oil slick that howls and moans and undulates with every impish crotch-thrust from their idols' plinths." Why would anyone voluntarily add themselves to this mindless, coagulated stain, when you can be "not like the other girls" instead? That's what I've always chosen.

Brené Brown would say the reason I squirm at the sight of the Cumberbitches isn't that I'm embarrassed; it's that I'm ashamed. They have put themselves out there, made themselves vulnerable and open to mockery. They have let themselves be seen, and to make myself feel better, I act like I'm cooler than that, when what I actually am is scared. I'm afraid to be seen. A lot of us have to "dig deep about the cool issue," she says.

I only know what Brené Brown would say about this because my best friend reads all her books and tells me about them. I'm too embarrassed to buy a self-help book. I'm not like the other middle-aged women.

❤

I SURPRISE MYSELF BY OPENING MY LAPTOP AGAIN, returning to the forum. I wish I could say I did this because I worked out that the fans on there were only a mirror to my own insecurities, but this is absolutely not the case. Do you really think this is the kind of story where people get over themselves that easily? Ha! No, it was because, despite myself, I just *had* to say something about the Post-it note. I couldn't stop thinking about it. I had found the golden ticket, but because no one in my life even knew I was borrowing books to look at pictures of Benedict Cumberbatch, there was no one I could gloat to. Except the people on the forum. I guess you could say I had nowhere else to go. I started typing. "So I found this note . . ." And they *were* happy for me. They were just as delighted as I was.

And why did I then arrange to meet up with the person who left the note, when that would necessitate a terrifying real-world interaction with a real-life Cumberbitch? Because if I squinted, it felt like it could almost be a normal-person catch-up rather than a fan gathering. There would only be the one of her, so, I calculated, the whirlpool probably wouldn't be strong enough to suck me in. And to be honest, it was also because she was *here*. Canberra is a city of only a few hundred thousand people. If you type "Is Canberra . . ." into Google, it will autofill with *Is Canberra a city?* (rude) and *Is Canberra boring?* (no, it's just that nothing ever, ever happens here). So when something does happen in Canberra, possibly by accident, then dammit, you go. When a powerful owl—basically just a big owl—took up short-term residence in a park, half of Canberra went to stand in that park and crane their necks up at the tree to look at it. It was on the news! The fact that someone else had even borrowed that *Sherlock* book from the library was amazing enough. That there were two people in Canberra with a thing for Benedict Cumberbatch, well, hold the front page! Just like with that owl, I had to go look. Finally something was happening.

Besides, I wouldn't tell anyone I was going. No one would have to know.

❤

DURING MY LUNCH BREAK AT WORK, I CYCLE OVER TO meet Jade at the café of the botanic gardens. It's a Friday and almost every other table is occupied by groups of older women who laugh with a very specific combination of conspiracy and outrage—leaning their heads together and then throwing them back—which I always associate with the sound of my mother's book club.

I know what Jade looks like because we've swapped

photos in the negotiations that have taken us from the note, to the forum, to email contact, to here. I'm sure she scrutinized my photo as carefully as I have hers: a family snap from a recent holiday to Southeast Asia. It reveals a small, gentle-looking woman but with the tense smile of someone who either doesn't like having her photo taken or has spent a fortnight cajoling her children across Southeast Asia. Or possibly both. At the café, we greet each other awkwardly, making jokes about blind dates.

It turns out that, in many ways, Jade is like me. She is around forty years old; she has a husband; she has two children; after university, she spent a number of years living overseas before settling in Canberra; she also struggled with her sense of self in motherhood, feeling stuck in the role of stay-at-home mom since stopping work to raise her kids. But these similarities are not why we fall into an instant intimacy.

In the glare of the midday sun, we giggle like old friends on a wine-soaked girls' night, intoxicated. Jade is the first person I speak to about Benedict Cumberbatch in the way that I want to—at length, in detail, with feeling. You might think there's a lot of Benedict Cumberbatch in this book, but you don't know the half of it. (Oh, that reminds me—have you seen that at the end of this book, there's an appendix entirely about Benedict Cumberbatch? I probably should have mentioned that earlier.)

Jade tells me she left the note in the library book to encourage more people to the forum during a lull in the *Sherlock* fandom induced by the long gaps between seasons. She hadn't considered that the note would result in real-world connection. Isolated by her domestic life, frustrated by her inability to get back into the workforce, Jade expresses herself on the internet, and it's a community where she feels at home. In the Benedict Cumberbatch fandom, she shares things she's written, pictures she's drawn, and information she's sourced about upcoming projects or productions under way. Jade is especially skilled at finding out information, a valuable currency. My friends and family often send me mentions of Benedict Cumberbatch they've found online, thinking—ludicrously—that I wouldn't have seen them already. For example, when this book is published, I guarantee you that someone will tell me about it. But Jade, she sources information I've never seen, from places I don't even know exist, from connections I don't even know how to make.

A one-track mind is usually seen as a bad thing, a deficiency, but a narrow outlet can generate enormous power, all that built-up energy funneled toward one point. And maybe that's a bad thing, but it feels like a good thing when I'm talking to Jade. If you had leaned over our café table to listen in on our chatter, it would have sounded shallow and one-dimensional, a lot of cringeworthy talk about some actor. But in this conversation, I feel more complete, more whole, than I have in years. (Sorry, kids, but it's true!) It's like every possible cubic centimeter on the interior of my body is finally in use. What a great trick, to feel so differently on the inside from how you appear on the outside, like a human TARDIS. Years later, another Benedict Cumberbatch fan would tell me that as she walks down the street, she looks at the other people, smiles to herself, and thinks, *If only you knew.* I get that completely: *If only you could see what's going on inside here. I'm so much more than you think.* I meet up with Jade again a few more times after that, at the café or at her house if her family is out. She is not weird, and in her company, I feel less weird. It's like we're both in on the trick.

You know how when you're in love with someone, all you want to do is talk about them endlessly, but no one else wants to because it's really boring? Imagine if someone wants to, and then multiply that someone by thousands or even tens of thousands. Jade opens up the depths and reaches of the Benedict Cumberbatch online fandom for me. She provides a human face for my dismissive caricatures of the forum users, a way in for me to see how alike we really are and how judgmental I've been. By following the links she sends me for Tumblr, Twitter, Reddit, and fanfiction sites, I start to discover even more people going through the same experience as me, and there are so many of them, all over the world.

A huge portion of these people are women, and women who are older than you think someone should be to fall in love with a celebrity. Like Lea said, "we're all thinking and feeling the exact same thing." Over and over again, I read about their shock and confusion that they have been "Cumberbatched," as the process is known. "I haven't felt this way since I was a teenager!" they say, dredging from their personal histories memories of lipstick kisses for Robert Smith, swoons for David Duchovny, or squeals for the Bee

Gees. Together we have ended up somewhere we never intended to go, attracted by a mysterious gravitational pull we don't really understand. I like it here. I like them. It's amazing how similar we all are, and not only because we are all inexplicably in love with Benedict Cumberbatch. That isn't even—and I can't believe I'm saying this—the most interesting thing about us; it's that we all seem so happy.

❤

ONE EVENING WHEN I'M AT JADE'S HOUSE, WATCHING Benedict Cumberbatch on her big TV, her husband calls from the camping trip he's on with the kids. We pause the show while she quickly chats with him. As Benedict Cumberbatch's frozen face looms over us from the wall, I can't help but notice that Jade's contribution to the phone conversation is very vague. There's no mention that she has company.

After she hangs up, I ask if her husband and kids know that I'm at their house, sitting on their couch, eating pizza. "No," Jade says, "I didn't tell them." In fact, she's never told them, or anyone else, anything about meeting up with me. No one in her real life even knows I exist. "I don't want anyone to know about any of this," she says, indicating my general direction. "They'll just say it's immature, silly fangirl stuff." She presses play on the remote and even though Benedict Cumberbatch's face is so big, I can't concentrate on him anymore. It's like the lights have been switched on, and I emerge from the darkness, blinking, to see us as we are: two middle-aged women—*mothers*—sitting on practical wipe-down sofas, gawping at this poor, unsuspecting man. It does not look good. When we finish the show, I scuttle out the door and get in the car.

On the drive home, I try to work out why I feel so wounded when, actually, Jade was just doing the same thing as me. I hadn't told anyone about her either; my visit was also timed to coincide with Nathan and the kids being away. But I think keeping a secret is very different from *being* the secret. One feels like necessary self-protection and the other feels like shame. It had been exciting, the hidden bond I had with her and all these other women online, our shared knowledge that we were more than we seemed. In the dark, we were alive. But now I realize, with the clarity that comes with minor mortification, that it's not a clever trick to keep your inner world invisible from the outside one. It's a trap. It splits you into your real and pretend self. And that's only attractive when Benedict Cumberbatch does it.

And it *is* silly fangirl stuff. What else could it be? The discovery of all these other women, all feeling the same thing, doesn't make it any better; it makes it worse, more stupid and more embarrassing. Maybe through safety in numbers you can, in private, feel validated and more normal—happy—but in the real world, *all these other women* is the cause of the problem. It's how the graph works! Jade knew what she was doing: unexpressed and unseen are how women's feelings hold the most value. Hidden inside library books, tucked away in online forums, at a girls' night in, dancing in the dark, if-only-you-knew, that's where they come alive. Send them into the real world and upon contact with light, they become the squeals of the Cumberbitches.

When Nathan and the kids got home from visiting his relatives later that night, I asked him how his trip went and said nothing about where I'd been. Instead, I started sending furtive messages, online, to the other people I'd found there. We were so happy. And nobody wants to see that.

part two

benediction

this is a chapter about holes

"How did I not know about this?"

Sophie, fifty-seven years old, returns home after her retail shift at the local shopping center, climbs the stairs of her old Queenslander house, goes into the tiny room that her husband and son helped to sound-proof, and closes the door behind her. She sits down in her comfortable desk chair, in front of a podcasting microphone, and opens up her recording software. Then, in her northern English accent, which has found its way to a hot and sweaty regional Queensland town, she records sentences like these:

You hold the door open and let him step inside. You're just bolting the lock and reaching for the light switch when he stops you. Fingers tangling with yours, he presses your hand to the wall. He's standing so close you can feel the warmth of his body seeping through your clothes. You brace yourself against the door, the keys in your hand clattering brightly against the wood. "I—" But you're not entirely sure what you wanted to say so you stop. Your knees buckle a little, bending to support yourself, your head falling forward as his left hand slides around your front to press itself to where your heart is thudding, thudding, thudding in the center of your chest.

It's fanfiction. The "you" in this story is Sherlock Holmes as played by Benedict Cumberbatch, and the "him" is John Watson. That's *Captain* John Watson to you, of the Fifth Northumberland Fusiliers, the canonical doctor and soldier. He's in uniform. I thought you might like to know that. This scene appears in chapter two of the story. In chapter four, you get to hear the thud of Captain Watson's beret hitting the floor. There are fifteen chapters.

Sophie didn't write this story; a fanfiction author called Ellipsical did. But Sophie is reading and recording it, so people can listen to it like it's an audiobook. Eighteen thousand people have already read that story online, and Sophie's audio version will increase that audience to include people wearing headphones, walking their dog, or doing the dishes. Or doing other things.

While she reads, her husband of twenty-five years is in the next room, and her sons too, if they're back home for a visit, watching TV perhaps. They know exactly what she's doing in there. Sophie has always been very open about it, even to her colleagues in the store where she works. In one survey of fanfiction readers and writers, only a quarter of respondents said they are comfortable with admitting to people in their "real life" that they consume explicit fanfiction, and Sophie is in that minority. She doesn't like hiding, or secrets. Shame isn't her thing. She was raised by her grandmother after her mother "got in the family way" at sixteen, thanks to the forty-year-old next-door neighbor. She's already been on the receiving end of enough shame to last a lifetime, thank you very much.

Sophie is one of the happy women I found online. Over the past five years, she's recorded over two hundred fifty podfics, as they're called, about half of which feature explicit sex scenes (if you google her username, Podfixx, you'll find her). At her peak, she was putting in thirty hours of work at her job and then another thirty hours at the microphone, every week. She does it, she says, because it pleases her. She loves the stories, and she loves when listeners write to her saying they felt they were really there with the characters, perched on the end of their bed. "I've got some really, really lovely listeners who I've made friends with," she says. "And, you know, I think the time has gone when internet friends were something to be sneered at or not taken seriously. You can make really good connections with people you meet on the internet because of a shared enjoyment."

In the real world, her family were very supportive with the technical setup, but that's the limit of their involvement. She doesn't know if they've listened to any of her recordings or read any fanfiction. They know where to find it, she says, and if they have delved into it, she's sure they'll never say.

"It's not me who's embarrassed. It's my husband!" she says. "He gets very embarrassed if you talk about anything sexual. If you put voice to it, he just goes silent. He literally shuts down. You can talk as much as you want but he won't say anything back." She's always loved doing amateur drama, and eight years ago she appeared in a local performance of *The Vagina Monologues*. "I mean, my husband knew it was *The Vagina Monologues*, but he didn't quite know what he was coming to. I was the character who had all the different orgasms on stage and I caught sight of him in the audience, and I swear to God, he was sitting there like"—she demonstrates what looks like a hedgehog rolled up into a ball, covering its head with its little feet—"going, 'Make her shut up!'"

Sophie laughs uproariously, and then continues. "I have to say that my husband has never once complained about anything I might have learned from fanfiction along the way. I don't wish to be indelicate, but he's never once gone, 'What are you doing?!' I might get an '*Oh!*'"—and now her hedgehog is bolt upright, eyes wide—"but he's never complained." She laughs so much she apologizes. "But it does give you license to try something different. You think, 'Hmm, that sounds like a good idea!'" She laughs again. And I'm writing "*she* laughs," but I'm also laughing so much throughout our conversation that when I listen back to the recording of our interview, I can barely hear anything above my wheezing. It sounds like a field recording from a bachelorette party with the Chippendales.

But that is the exact opposite of what goes on in her studio, soundproofed with patterned duvet covers hung on the ceiling and walls, and silent except for her own gentle, lilting voice. "It's the mark of a good writer who can write a good sex scene, that it's the kind of thing that draws you in. It has you going '*Oof.*' And it's that *oof* feeling where, you know, you kind of think, *I'll just go for a little lie-down*—without being coarse about it. And it's the funniest things that can make me feel like that. It's just, you know, certain words like: 'He moaned.' That can have me like a puddle of goo. *Oof.* And if I can make anybody *oof* through my reading, then I just think, *Well, that's the job done.*"

It's a job, she says, to be done alone. "Put it this way: if I got a passage up now and tried to read it to you, I'd be beside myself with embarrassment. I couldn't even listen back to this interview without cringing. It's like when you see yourself on a video and you cover your eyes and go, 'Oh God, oh God.' Yet if I think nobody's listening and it's just me and a microphone, and I'm enjoying the story, that's different. If I think that I could be overheard by anybody, that would be awful. That would be absolutely crushing." She pauses. "Isn't that strange?"

❤

FANFICTION IS ONE OF THE THINGS THAT JADE INTRO-duced me to. Until then, I had no idea that it existed. Or maybe I had a vague idea that *Fifty Shades of Grey* started life as *Twilight* fanfiction, but I didn't know what that actually meant. I just knew that it somehow mixed teenage girls with middle-aged romance readers, which sounded like a sickly cocktail I did not want to try. But Jade talked me through it, and now I can guide you too. Only if you need a guide, of course. If you don't, if you already know all about it, maybe you could use this time to revisit the memory of what it was like for you when you first found fanfiction. A little while ago, I saw a news story about a woman living in a New York apartment who discovered an entire other, hidden apartment behind her bathroom mirror, and isn't that just what it's like? A completely new thing you never knew about, which was there the whole time. And then all of a sudden, you have so much more space to move around in than you ever realized.

Fanfiction is, as you would expect, fiction written by fans, which connects in some way to a preexisting cultural or media product. It might feature characters from a TV show, or a movie, or a book, or a comic, or they could even be sports stars or musicians or gamers or politicians who exist in real life. The extent to which the fanfiction leans on the original work or characters varies enormously, with some stories simply rewriting a show's ending, for example, while others might take inspiration from the show's characters but completely rewrite the universe they exist in.

The BBC version of *Sherlock* is a kind of fanfiction itself, placing Sir Arthur Conan Doyle's Holmes and Watson in a modern London setting, and making them look like Benedict Cumberbatch and Martin Freeman. Why stop there, when you can then make those characters do whatever you want, to whomever you want, wherever you want, in other fanfiction? Why not take the Benedict Cumberbatch and Martin Freeman versions of Sherlock and John, but make them be a barista and customer at your local coffee shop, or wizards at Hogwarts, or cowboys in the *Brokeback Mountain* universe? Many stories just like these already exist, and many of them are extremely good too. This is the case with a lot of fanfiction (often shortened to "fic"), although as in any bookshop, the quality of the writing varies.

Unlike traditionally published fiction, there's no gatekeeping to becoming a fic author. You just post your story on a site like Archive of Our Own or Wattpad or fanfiction.net. Sure, you won't get paid but you'll get real-time feedback from a potential readership of such magnitude that it would make a debut novelist weep. Archive of Our Own receives over 14 million unique visitors a month; during the COVID-19 lockdown, there was one particular Sunday when the site clocked 68.6 million page views in twenty-four hours. There are currently around 7 million stories on the platform, spread across forty thousand different fandoms. So really, it's less like discovering an empty three-bedroom apartment behind your bathroom mirror and more like stumbling upon a heaving metropolis.

It is categorically not true to say all fanfiction is erotic. On Archive of Our Own, only about a third of the stories are rated Mature or Explicit, and on fanfiction.net and Wattpad, it's even less than that. But it *is* true to say that almost all fanfiction, across all platforms, does involve a romantic or sexual relationship of some kind, which is called "shipping." Of all the shipping that goes on, far and away the most popular type is a ship that involves men paired together (hello, Captain Watson), categorized as male/male or "slash" in the parlance of fanfiction. The pairing between Benedict Cumberbatch's Sherlock Holmes and Martin Freeman's John Watson is one of the most popular pairings in fic on Archive of Our Own.

But unlike these fictional men who are in love with other fictional men, almost all of the real-life people writing and reading these male/male stories are not cisgender men. In an Archive of Our Own user survey, there were more respondents who identified as genderqueer than who identified as male (less than 4 percent); 80 percent of respondents identified as women. So it's like discovering a metropolis filled with a lot of people who don't identify as cisgender men, imagining relationships between people who do. Isn't that strange?

❤

SOPHIE RECALLS THE TIME SHE FIRST DELVED INTO AN erotic fic, and listening to it is like getting a front-row seat at *The Vagina Monologues*. "In the first instance, I was shocked at the explicitness of it and the language used. I was also shocked that it stirred me, I suppose. I was just sitting there, openmouthed, like, oh my *God*. No. Oh no. Surely not. No . . . *really*? Well, maybe? Ye-es? Yes. *Yes!*"

I remember Jade telling me about fic and thinking that the idea of Sherlock Holmes getting into bed with John Watson seemed kind of unnecessary. It would never happen in the show, so why take the characters down that path? I may even have said, "Why does everything always have to be about sex?" in a great, if unintentional, impersonation of my mother.

(I can't let this moment pass without noting that the opposite problem occurs when it comes to the literary source material for *Sherlock*. Okay, so sex does not figure prominently in the BBC series, but I challenge you *not* to think about it while reading the original Conan Doyle detective stories, thanks to the sheer number of times Watson "ejaculates" at Holmes. In *The Adventures of the Resident Patient*, you'll even find the most perfect five-word erotic story ever written: "'My dear Holmes!' I ejaculated." There's also a particularly great scene in "The Man with the Twisted Lip" involving a "heap of shag.")

While many people—including, importantly, many LGBTQIA+ people—have detected sexual tension between the main characters in *Sherlock*, Jade agreed that it hadn't been particularly obvious to her either, but, she added, "There's actually some pretty good writing about it." And, what can I say? There *is* some pretty good writing about it. So good that it became instantly irrelevant to me whether that sexual tension was present, either intentionally or accidentally, in the show. "You can't kill an idea, can you?" Sherlock Holmes says in one episode. "Not once it's made a home *there*," and he taps Detective Inspector Lestrade's forehead. My forehead had been well and truly tapped.

If Sophie's first experience of explicit fic is the kind of vocal performance you'd expect from a podficcer, mine is the kind of mime you'd expect from a mother trying not to wake the napping children. My jaw dropped, and I lifted my eyes up from my phone to do one of those *are-you-seeing-this?* sweeps of the room. No one else was there, but I was searching for a witness to corroborate what was happening. *Can you believe it?* I wanted to say. And then, shaking them by the shoulders: *Did you know about this?*

How did I not know about this? And by "this," I don't mean fanfiction itself. There's a lot of things on the internet I don't know about, which is not surprising at all. No, I mean, how did I not know about *this*: the way fanfiction made me feel. How did someone, out there, know what would tick my boxes so precisely, when I didn't? I could read different versions of essentially the same relationship over and over again, each time as shocked and thrilled as if it were my first encounter. *They're just friends! Or is there something more? So much is unspoken! Pining! Angst! Someone's hurt! They need looking after! OMG there's only one bed! They're cold! They have to huddle! He moaned! Argh, they loved each other all along!* Put them in Hogwarts, put them on horses, put them in space, I didn't care. In one survey on fanfiction users, 80 percent said they have an "endless appetite" for their favorite ship, and I can only agree with them. Speaking of ships, put them on a ship! Rear Admiral John Watson? Sign me up! But with a lot of terms and conditions, like, don't mention it to anyone, and also, please tell me what the hell is going on with me.

Don't you think it's a bit weird that when you're dreaming, you can scare yourself? Really, how can you not know that someone's going to leap out from behind the bushes, when it's you who put them there? Conscious, unconscious, Freud, something something? I guess it's the same thing with desires. They similarly exist inside you but can still take you by surprise. In any case, it's quite discombobulating to discover you're into something you never knew was there. You want an explanation. "I've thought about this an awful lot," Sophie says. "Why would a middle-aged straight woman—and I mean, I do identify as being bisexual, but I've been married to my husband for years so for all intents and purposes, I'm straight—why would a middle-aged straight woman find sexual enlightenment or sexual pleasure in reading about homosexual relationships between these two men? I struggled with that for a little while."

"OOC" is something you'll sometimes see people write in the comments of a fic. It's shorthand for "out of character." It means the character in the story isn't behaving the way they should, based on what we know about them. "OOC" is often given as a piece of negative feedback. We don't like it when someone acts out of character.

My *oof* was OOC. And I didn't like it. Well, I liked the *oof*. I didn't like the struggle, as Sophie calls it, of squaring this pleasure with how I saw myself. I hadn't even begun to come to terms with being in love with a man on the television, and now I was imagining him doing unspeakable things to his flatmate at 221B Baker Street. What next? I start publishing anonymous fanfiction of my own?! HAHA-HAHA. I felt extremely uncomfortable with this character (me); she wasn't behaving the way I expected. Do you remember when Kyndall told the psychologist that she had an abundance of sexual energy? *This* is what she was talking about. "What is happening to me?" she wanted to know.

❤

WHEN I WAS IN YEAR 6, I WAS INVITED TO A SLEEPOVER with a group of friends, which was not the kind of thing that happened to me very often. Obviously, I went. We were in our pajamas, watching *Beverly Hills, 90210*, when Rebecca and Caitlin, the popular twins from my class (Rebecca had the bangs so you could tell them apart), started making comments about Jason Priestley and how he made your tummy feel all funny, right? "I know!" all the girls said, including me because I'm excellent at pretending I'm just like everyone else, but really I was thinking, *Wait—he does* <u>what</u>?

I spent the following summer holidays, the one before starting junior high, dutifully cutting out photos of Jason Priestley from *TV Hits* and sticking him to the cover of my new school diary, right next to his castmates Luke Perry and Brian Austin Green. Edward Furlong was there too, and Christian Slater, River Phoenix, and Keanu Reeves. None of them had managed to spark this fabled feeling in my stomach, but with their strong jawlines and smoldering eyes, they would deliver a unified message to anyone who looked at them. *The bearer of this document is a standard-issue girl. Nothing to see here. Move on.*

This was before Michael Hutchence, for anyone tracking

the timeline of famous white men in my life. But he was different anyway. I actually liked Michael Hutchence, which is why I kept my feelings about him secret. These inert heartthrobs on my diary were just props for a twelve-year-old girl trying to look thirteen. I didn't care about them—I thought "Keanu" was pronounced *Kee-nu*!—and that hardly mattered, because they were cutouts in every sense: mere stand-ins for desire.

The following summer, I tossed that school diary, tatty after a year of wear and tear, but something about it stayed with me (not Brian Austin Green—sorry, Brian). I worked out what Rebecca and Caitlin meant about the funny feeling in your stomach, but I didn't take that opportunity to then investigate what, for me, brought this on. I just repeated the same process as before, looking around for source material that seemed to represent the performance of this feeling. I cast aside *TV Hits* and turned to the bikini babe GIFs I found on my brother's computer. Do you know how long it took, in the midnineties, for a GIF to load? I had more than enough time to scrutinize every pixel, studying what I should be into, turning over my fantasies to someone else's imagination. From the very beginning, my desires were only ever in relation to someone else's; none of them began with "I."

Adolescent girls, Ariel Levy writes in *Female Chauvinist Pigs*, are pressured to *seem* sexy. The result is that they "have a very difficult time learning to recognize their own sexual desire, which would seem a critical component of *feeling* sexy." This is not without consequence, as the anthropologist

Katherine Rowland found. She interviewed over one hundred women for her book *The Pleasure Gap*, observing that many straight women, in particular, have failed to consider, at a fundamental level, the nature and object of their desires. In contrast, Rowland writes, queer women report having fewer sexual problems than heterosexual women, as well as being more easily aroused and more sexually assertive. In terms of pleasure and satisfaction, she writes, queer women have an advantage, albeit hard-won: marginalization, or the need to "come out" as anything other than the default "norm," can compel you to attend more closely to your desires, whether you want to or not.

Rowland observes that the heterosexual women in her interviews don't seem to know how to access their erotic delight. They "hold themselves back." They "condemn their fantasies, foreclose on what they really want, and sell themselves short on the idea that sex and love must look a certain way." These women need to liberate their erotic imagination, Rowland suggests, by sensing "an internal flicker of *I want that*"—whatever *that* may be—"and feeling empowered to act accordingly."

Over half of the users on Archive of Our Own identify as a gender, sexual, or romantic minority, and it's not at all "strange" that these readers are drawn to the depiction of gay relationships prevalent in fanfiction, regardless of the genders of the characters involved. What is *strange*, however, is how hard it is for straight, cisgender women, like me, to imagine desire—our own, as well as anyone else's—looking in any way different from the picture we've been sold and, apparently, bought into wholesale.

I don't presume to think that fanfiction is everyone's cup of tea, and even if it is, you shouldn't feel obliged to tell anyone about it. I don't think it's anyone else's business what goes on in your mind. But if you stepped into Sophie's little soundproofed room and sat down in her comfy chair, with no one listening in, and if you were truly unseen, and truly unheard, what would you actually *want*? What if you don't even know?

♥

"SO WHAT DO YOU THINK IT'S ALL ABOUT?" SOPHIE ASKS me. We'd just been talking about the fantasy element of fic, and how that bleeds into the everyday, but not necessarily in a sexual way. "I'll be doing the banking in the morning and all of a sudden I would think, 'I wonder what Benedict Cumberbatch is doing right now?'" Sophie says. "Why is that?" she asks. "Do you think that it's tied up with some kind of lack in our real lives?"

I feel well-equipped to answer the question, because I'd just read a book on this subject, called *By Force of Fantasy*. The author, psychoanalyst Ethel S. Person, says that fantasy—daydreaming, reverie, the playing out of mental scripts, as well as sexual fantasy—is no idle pursuit. It serves a valuable role in our lives, soothing us, arousing us, and shaping us as people. That's why it's important to pay attention to our fantastical thoughts, she says, even if they sometimes feel embarrassing or shameful. They still affect our real lives, "sometimes in the direction of radical change."

Because we rarely divulge our fantasies, Person continues, we miss out on the opportunity to properly evaluate them. We don't get to hear what other people think, and we don't discover who else shares them. Sometimes our fantasy life becomes so secret or forbidden that we start to hide it even from ourselves. "Many adults who in their early years spent a considerable amount of time in the realm of the imagination may, with the responsibilities of adulthood or the disappointment of failed dreams, cease to pay much attention to the inner channel," she says. "Out of self-protection, they eliminate fantasy." We lie in bed, trying to get to sleep, thinking about our to-do list, because to consider an alternate life, even in fantasy, is too hard to bear.

I think about Sophie's question, and whether daydreaming about Benedict Cumberbatch suggests something's missing from our real life. A "lack" makes it sound like we're using it as a kind of crutch, but it feels more like tapping into something than compensating for it. "I think it fills a hole you don't know is there, until you fill it," I offer, and we immediately start tittering over how it sounds. "Like one of your erotic stories!" I ejaculate. "But no," Sophie replies, "there's nothing erotic about not having any fanfic. That's just a hole."

Sophie begins to ponder this scenario. "I would feel genuinely bereft if I didn't have access to all these pleasurable things I currently have. What would I *do* with my life?" She sounds horrified at the thought. "How would I flipping fill it? What would I want to do instead, if I couldn't swing my microphone around?" But Sophie is thinking only of the hole suddenly being emptied, which I don't think is a thing that happens. It's more likely for the hole never to be explored at all. How *can* it be, if you don't even know it's there?

Or there's this: you do know about the hole, but you stop yourself from filling it, out of self-protection.

chapter eight

this is a chapter about what matters

"i get trapped in creating meaning."

Fanfiction is when things really started to go off the rails for me. I had run out of Benedict Cumberbatch movies and TV shows to watch, which was a frustrating roadblock to my insatiable cravings. So imagine how it felt to then tap into an almost bottomless well of new material that, even at my obsessive rate of consumption, would seemingly never run dry. There are over 120,000 *Sherlock* fics on Archive of Our Own. There are 3,500 fics inspired by a *radio comedy* Benedict Cumberbatch did. I'm licking my lips just thinking about it.

Back at the beginning of all this, this thing between me and Benedict Cumberbatch, the badness of it felt physiological, a malfunction in my chemistry, my biology, my wiring, over which I had no control. What could I do? [Throws hands into air.] He's a good-lookin' guy! But when I started reading and—uh-oh—enjoying fanfiction, the badness of it changed. Now, it was a personal failing. There was no getting around the fact that I was reading fic intentionally. It wasn't "happening to me," like the way Benedict Cumberbatch would appear in my mind unbidden. I was making it happen. I was getting better and better at choosing stories I knew I would like, finessing my searches to hit exactly the right spots, and I was making those rational, considered choices, over and over again.

As I found myself clicking to open another tab on Archive of Our Own, I would mutter, "I *hate* that I love this." Even Sophie, who loves to love fanfiction, says that she has wondered sometimes whether reading and voicing stories with the same characters over and over again is really stretching herself. "I don't know, maybe I've ended up being very narrow," she says. What would be a better use of your time? I ask her, and in her best queen's English, she replies, "Oh, I suppose reading the classics, *darling*, and broadening one's mind."

Sophie is very funny, but she's *rather* hit the nail on the head, hasn't she? Fanfiction is not considered a good use of a person's time or mind. And there's a certain shame in that. In terms of stigmatization, fanfiction ranks below even the much-maligned genre of romance. Romance novels are trashed mercilessly (which is entirely unfair), but at least they're part of a billion-dollar industry. Fanfiction has no economic value. It is amateur, illegitimate. It is formulaic in many ways, often repetitive, and, by its very nature, derivative. "Fanfiction is to writing what a cake mix is to gourmet cooking," the science fiction writer Robin Hobb once said. And then, on a bit of a roll, she also said: "Fanfiction is an Elvis impersonator who thinks he is original." And now, wow, the metaphors were just flowing out of her: "Fanfiction is paint-by-number art."

I could see with my own eyes that the fanfiction I was reading was better than many published novels, and I could feel in my, er, gut that I was enjoying it, but I also could not shake the feeling that it was making me dumber. I don't know how I ended up being such a snob. My postmodern media studies degree—in which we actually studied *Die Hard* as a serious text, twice—was supposed to make me appreciate the value of "low" culture. Yet I've never been able to shake the idea that there's a good reason why some things are called "guilty pleasures." *Die Hard* is a perfectly enjoyable object of study, but not one I'm *proud* of. Similarly, my heart might have yearned for more and more fanfiction, but that didn't mean I should feel happy about it.

Sophie, perhaps sensing that she's dealing with a bad case of Bruce Willis–induced intellectual insecurity, says she knows exactly who I need to speak to about this: Emma. She's a fic writer, but she's also a professor of some kind. This is excellent news. I don't know who I thought was writing all these stories, but it wasn't professors. A professor could give fic the kind of endorsement that would make everything (including me) seem okay.

❤

WHEN SHE JOINS THE VIDEO CALL, EMMA IS EXACTLY what I was hoping for. She is on her campus in Canada, in an office crowded with boxes and papers. She wears glasses and uses her hands constantly to emphasize her points—just like in a lecture! She tells me she's a humanities professor, specializing in medieval literature, in the process of retiring, but still currently working. Her husband is an academic too. It's all perfect. At one point, Emma refers to me as a "literary critic," which is 100 percent inaccurate, but I don't correct her, because I'm super into it. Plus, I'm sure I could be, if it hadn't been for all that *Die Hard*.

"I don't mean to imply that you don't already know this," Emma says, as she starts describing how fanfiction would be right at home in the Middle Ages (I do not already know this). I have asked her, as a professor, to explain why fic is as valid as any other literature, and a good use of a smart person's time. I want her imprimatur so I can mount a stirring defense as to why being a fanfiction-reading Cumberbitch is a legit thing. I want it to be like when someone asked Stephen Hawking about the cosmological impact of Zayn Malik leaving One Direction and he answered it seriously. "Finally a question about something important," he said, before explaining that one day theoretical physics might prove that universes exist outside our own, where Zayn could still be in the band. What a gift that was for the Directioners! I want that. And Emma delivers.

"Medieval authors never thought, 'What can I write that is wholly original and uniquely mine?' Because nobody would want to read that," she says. "They wanted to read about the characters they knew and loved and that were in popular circulation. You would never see a medieval reader or writer saying, 'Oh, no! Not another story about King Arthur and his knights.' It's more like, '*King Arthur and his knights!*'" she says, breathlessly, hands clutched to her chest, eyes wide. Wanting more and more from the same characters wasn't invented in the Middle Ages, either. It's not hard to reimagine Greek tragedy as a kind of fanfiction, with ancient gods and goddesses appearing over and over again to explore permutations of the same themes for adoring audiences.

The age of print is what changed everything, Emma says. It was bad news for King Arthur stans. "When it was a matter of being able to make large sums of money from multiple copies that only your imprimery could print, that's when creativity began to be defined in terms of *originality*—or rather, that originality began to be defined as absolute novelty. There's this wonderful phrase from a scholar of Old French, about what originality meant in the Middle Ages. It's about a French poet—named Rutebeuf—and she says, originality, or total innovation, ex nihilo, was not interesting to medieval people. What they valued as original was the 'creative recombination of inherited materials.' I love that phrase, because that is fic: the creative recombination of inherited materials." And I love this conversation. It has *Latin* in it.

When you go to the extremely heteronormative Wikipedia page for the "thinking woman's crumpet," there's a photo of one man and one man only and it's Benedict Cumberbatch. (Okay, yes, there's also a photo of one woman and one woman only and that's Helen Mirren, because the page is shared with the "thinking man's crumpet." Got to give Helen her due.) It's a good photo of Benedict Cumberbatch—the tilt of his head providing perfect visual harmony between cheekbone and jawline—so you may as well keep the page open, just to get another glimpse of it while you're looking up meanings of Latin phrases.

Anyway, he's the crumpet, and I'm the *thinking* woman, and that means a lot to me. A celebrity crush might be ipso facto pretty dumb, but at least if your crush is on Benedict Cumberbatch (or, I guess, Helen Mirren), you're making the best of a bad situation. And I'm certain that with Emma offering up all the learned ammunition I need to hold my ground, I'll be able to *think* my way into it being an actual good situation. Crumpets for everyone!

Emma says there is no reason for a thinking woman to be ashamed of fandom, or fanfiction, at all. "I am shameless," she says, laughing. But then she says that she still keeps her fic-writing secret from her colleagues, which is a bit confusing. "I'm shameless—but closeted," she clarifies. "Having people know that I write fic, or if they read what I write, I am absolutely convinced would reflect on the way they would evaluate my scholarship." She doesn't care what her colleagues think about fanfiction as a category, or whether they think she's slumming it with lowbrow, paint-by-number art or whatever. As a literary historian, she says she's worked through all those issues before: "Half the stuff I adore from the Middle Ages is the equivalent of comic books." It's more about not wanting to cross the streams between fic and her work, she says, and protecting her academic mask. "It's the whole cloak-of-infallibility thing, you know?"

"Hmm, okay," I say, and I ask her to explain.

Posturing and posing is a big part of academia, she says. You have to wear a mask of neutrality, and a cloak of infallibility, especially if you're a woman in a male-dominated field. It's a culture where "you don't admit allegiance or love for anything, because the pose everyone wants to occupy is being smarter than their text." You might have originally entered academia because of your passionate love for the discipline, but if you want to get anywhere, you have to learn to hide that passion. "There's this kind of implied pressure to conceal that love in order to look like you don't have any blind spots on the defects of your object of study."

It is, Emma says, a particularly masculine approach to expertise. "I don't want to generalize, but the fact that men, in the cultures I know best, are encouraged to quash the emotional dimension of their lives is something that makes me say, sure, male academics love their stuff, but I'm not sure they're even aware of it. They think of the love they have for their discipline as a balanced and nuanced appreciation of the virtuous or the valuable. Do you know what I mean?" I do, because it's not just in academia. It's the men at the concerts. "They have to perform a certain kind of straight masculinity which requires you to be able to say that other people are emotional, not you." Ah yes, other people: the girls at the concerts.

"That is something I grew really weary of," Emma says, and she sounds weary, "because my one superpower as a teacher, and I only have one, is the absolute adoration for the stuff I teach. When I teach Chaucer, in those moments, I am utterly convinced there is *nothing* else so worthy of our time and attention in this world as *The Canterbury Tales*. So it never fit my personality very well to say, 'Well, of *course* we have to be aware that Chaucer blah blah blah . . .'" And she transforms into an impression of puffed-up pomposity. "Academia is so afraid of being dewy-eyed and idealistic right now that they have gone straight over into stink-eye, the hermeneutic of suspicion, of cynical jadedness.

"And I became tired," she says, and she sounds tired, "of even pretending to be balanced on the subject of monuments of medieval literature that I love so much. This is one of the reasons I was so glad to retire." Then she asks me, "Do you remember that film *The Madness of King George*?" And I say yes, even though I don't. "At the end of the film, when the king is again in a state of mind that is lucid, he says something like, 'I always knew who I was; I had just forgotten how to *seem.*'

"At the end of my career, I was so tired of seeming." How

to seem detached. How to seem above it all. "I hadn't forgotten how to do it, but I didn't *want* to do it anymore."

In the final five years of her academic career, Emma found herself writing little scenes and pieces of dialogue based on *Sherlock*, a show she had become heavily invested in; maybe she'd even fallen in love. Amid her sixty- to eighty-hour working weeks, she'd scribble words on scraps of paper that she'd tuck into notebooks, waiting until she was ready to write them up into proper stories. The first fic she would eventually publish on Archive of Our Own was novel length.

When Emma was twelve, she and a friend wrote stories about *Star Trek*—she remembers their loopy, girlish handwriting on the yellow legal pads they passed back and forth—and she says she feels like she has more in common, now, with that twelve-year-old girl than with the professor she has seemed to become. Those stories were fanfiction too, of course; she just didn't know it. In fanfiction, it might be impossible to love something too much; neutrality, objectivity, posturing, these things can't get much purchase when the essential generative fuel is passion.

"It is just sheerly for fun," Emma says of fandom. "It is grace freely given. It is joy shared without consideration of compensation or payback." To her, it's the opposite of work; it's play. "Once we're adults, we relinquish play far too thoroughly. The so-called Protestant work ethic is a total rip-off." Fandom is about reclaiming that play space for "productive selfishness," she says, and "the assignment of your time according to whatever the fuck you feel like, instead of what would be most efficient, or most advantageous to others. It's as important to me as eating healthy or getting exercise, but it's not some kind of dreary obligation. It's just utter delight."

I've still got that Wikipedia page open, the one for the thinking woman's crumpet. I'm looking at that photo right now. It's not research, I have no excuse to be here. I just love looking at it. So why do I need a cover story? Why isn't Benedict Cumberbatch, prima facie, worthy of my time and attention? "Beating oneself up for what really gets you excited, it's a masculine approach to women's experiences," Emma says. "We have been acculturated to do it to ourselves."

❤

SOME YEARS AGO NOW, A CANBERRA WOMAN NAMED Elizabeth Caplice started a blog to document her terrible experience with cancer. I didn't know her personally, but her story has stayed with me, as I'm sure it has for many of her other readers. In one of her posts, Elizabeth writes, "i get trapped in creating meaning," and I think about that phrase a lot. In the post, she goes on to say how the nurse who's looking after her "often has to just tell me that it's ok if all i want to do is sit around and watch *The Hunger Games* movies or re-watch *Star Trek*, and that i don't need to spend every moment engaging with the world. she told me that watching *The Hunger Games* is meaningful because through doing this, i am taking my mind off things, or enjoying myself, or whatever it is we do when we watch trashy movies or TV that we like, and that this is ok. i don't need to be in this mindful and meditative zone where all i do is feel profound about my observations about life and death."

Making meaning no longer held any sense to her anyway, Elizabeth wrote: "i am hoping to just be alive, just that little bit longer." She died three months later, just after her thirty-second birthday. Her birthday cake had Patrick Stewart as Captain Picard on it.

My thoughts circle back to this post all the time, for many different reasons. One of them is to wonder what I would do if, like Elizabeth, I had only a few months to live. Would I want to use my time to look at Benedict Cumberbatch?

Then usually, like a call-and-response impulse, straight after thinking about that blog post, I remember these lines from the most quotable of poets, Mary Oliver: "Tell me, what is it you plan to do / with your one wild and precious life?" That quote is all over the Instagram feeds of women my age, tormenting us with its accusatory tone. What is it *I* plan to do? I don't know, you tell me! Seriously, what could stand up to this test, of being worth the expenditure of my *one wild and precious life*? Half of it is already over! What could possibly matter enough? I always assumed the answer was supposed to be something about your family, your loved ones, your children. But then I had kids, and I couldn't figure out how to make that work either. It was always when I was on my hands and knees, again, wiping the crumbs and gunk off the mat under the high chair, again, that these words weighed on me the heaviest. *Tell me, Tabitha*, I would think, *is* this *what you plan to do with your one wild and precious life?* Not even children can make that much meaning.

When Mary Oliver died not that long ago, and she was being quoted everywhere, even more than usual, I was prompted to look up the rest of that poem, which is called "The Summer Day." It turns out I had it completely and utterly wrong, which is very embarrassing for a literary critic. "The Summer Day" isn't about finding your Big Purpose at all! It's about kneeling down in the grass, and looking very, very closely at a *grasshopper*, and doing nothing more with your time than strolling through fields, being idle. Before she gets to the question about your one wild and precious life, Mary Oliver actually asks something else of the reader first: "Tell me, what else should I have done?" How could she have made better use of her day than lying in the grass with the grasshopper? "Doesn't everything die at last, and too soon?" And there's nothing to be done about it, except to pay attention to what moves us, in this, our one wild and precious life. And that is a very different poem.

Does it matter what it is that moves us, so long as we are moved? If it's a grasshopper, or *The Canterbury Tales*, or *Star Trek*, or Benedict Cumberbatch? Mary Oliver probably wasn't a big fan of Benedict Cumberbatch, but she clearly didn't believe in beating yourself up over what gets you excited. And I know it's a bad idea to reduce poetry to inspirational quotes, but if you look at another of her most famous poems, "Wild Geese," you'll find that Mary Oliver helpfully offers an answer to the vexing question of what could actually be worth our one wild and precious life: "You only have to let the soft animal of your body / love what it loves." It sounds so easy.

Tell me, do you know what it is that you love? Not who—I already know you love the most important people in your life—but what. And if you didn't have to explain or defend it, would that change anything for you? I'm not implying you're harboring an unspoken passion for something deeply embarrassing, although if you are, then you're in the right place. But have you made yourself available to love the full suite of things that might move you? Or has the soft animal of your body been cut off at the pass, diverted toward things that seem more important? If, like the nurse in Elizabeth Caplice's blog post, I told you it was okay, that not everything needs to be about making meaning, that not everything has to be justifiable as a good use of your time or mind, could you then let the soft animal of your body find its way toward loving what it loves? And what would that look like for you? It's not that easy.

❤

EMMA HAS TO GO, AND I AM ANNOYED AT MYSELF. I asked her so many questions about the Middle Ages (?!), to try to prove how smart I am, when clearly her real expertise lies elsewhere, on the subject of love, and utter delight, and doing whatever the fuck you want. I came to her for the wrong kind of validation. Why should anyone care about the opinion of a theoretical physicist on the subject of One Direction? Why is that worth more than the demonstrable, all-consuming love felt by millions of girls?

I realize that I too am tired of *seeming*. It's exhausting. I'm tired of always trying to stay one step ahead of perceived criticism. I'm tired of the second-guessing, the diagnosing, the explaining, the hiding, the talking about what it all *means*. I'm tired of seeming like someone who wouldn't fall in love with Benedict Cumberbatch; or someone who has—okay, you got me!—fallen in love with Benedict Cumberbatch but *knowingly*. He should be called "the overthinking woman's crumpet," as far as I'm concerned. And I can either continue to hate that I love him, which is getting really boring, or try loving to love him, which still seems weirdly hard.

In an excellent essay for *Catapult* magazine about fanfiction (which is really an excellent essay about love), the writer Emilia Copeland Titus notes, "Indifference is easy, but love—the kind of love that runs so deep and so clear that it threatens to burst the dam of your heart—is difficult." It's true. "There will always be people who expect you to explain that love," she continues, "and that is perhaps the biggest challenge of all, even for those whose careers are dedicated to explaining and describing ideas." But eventually, holding back that dam-bursting love gets tiring. And then, there's only one thing for it: "Let the floodgates open."

If I had months to live, I would use that time to love Benedict Cumberbatch. Not *all* that time, of course, but as much of it as I wanted. I would even keep looking at pictures of him on the internet. Ridiculous, hey? It is not a good use of my time or mind, and it does not matter, and yet, there you have it. How could I ever justify this—wasting my precious time on something so unimportant? I can't, not according to the criteria we use for deciding such things, anyway. That yardstick only measures stuff like productivity, objectivity, legitimacy, appropriateness. It doesn't take into consideration, at all, how my love for something as silly as Benedict Cumberbatch makes me feel, and what that's worth to me. It's someone else's value system, one that sees loving something, and especially loving something *too much*, as a bad thing, a problem, an embarrassment. It's a system that doesn't know how to account for all the ways in which other people might make meaning. On this measure, my love for Benedict Cumberbatch is never going to cut it, no matter how hard I try. And I'm tired of trying.

If I had months to live, I would want to use that time to do what I love. After all, what could be more worthy of my time and attention than that?

There's just one more thing to sort out. I tell Emma, "Please, wait, I have to ask another question, my last one," before she disappears back into her university campus.

chapter nine

this is a chapter about other people

"What does your husband think about all this?"

You want to know what my husband thinks about all this. That's okay, you're not the only one. In fact, I am asked the question so often that I have had to develop a stock response to deflect it. "He knows that good things come to those whose wives are obsessed with Benedict Cumberbatch," I say. It's so icky that few dare to continue their line of questioning for fear of what/who might come next.

It's a recurring problem for Benedict Cumberbatch as well. "I have boyfriends coming up to say, 'My girlfriend is obsessed with you,'" he told *Vogue*, "and I say, 'I'm so sorry.'" Benedict Cumberbatch is sorry, and I'm sorry too. We're sorry for what we're doing to the boyfriends and the husbands. We know it doesn't look good for them, to be cuckolded by Bendy Dick Cum On My Baps, as he was apparently known at school.

At this point, I have spoken to a lot of people with a thing for Benedict Cumberbatch, many of whom are married, heterosexual women. There usually comes a time in the conversation when, having talked about nothing other than Benedict Cumberbatch for an hour or so, they assure me that despite how it may sound, they actually do love their husbands. (Although there was that woman in Western Australia who seemed to love Benedict Cumberbatch almost to *spite* her husband. "When he's giving me the shits," she told me, "I just say, bugger this, and I go read some gay fanfiction." An icon. A legend.) One woman, talking to me over the phone, cupped the receiver when she heard her husband come in the front door. "This is the kind of conversation I try not to have in the *marital* home," she whispered.

"Why?" I replied, also whispering, unnecessarily.

Because, she said, her relationship with Benedict Cumberbatch is akin to "an affair of the mind."

"Is it?!" I hissed back, now very stressed about my own marital home. I'd just finished reading a *New Yorker* story about British explorer Henry Worsley's all-consuming obsession with walking across Antarctica. My conclusion was that "crossing things" is a type of obsession I'll never be able to understand. Anyway, in the article, I was struck by how Worsley's very supportive wife, Joanna, referred to Antarctica as her husband's "mistress." I suppose if you can cheat on your spouse with a chilly continent, then, yes, you can cheat on your spouse with a celebrity you've never met. Then there's that thing where women describe themselves as "football widows" during the appropriate seasons. Here, football isn't the other woman but the cause of death: the murderer, even. A mind affair seems pretty tame by comparison. In any case, it's clearly possible for a passion to get in the way of a relationship.

The woman on the phone asks to remain completely anonymous before saying goodbye. She'd said she's not ashamed about her feelings for Benedict Cumberbatch, but at one point she'd also said that when she wakes up in the morning and turns on the computer to look at photos of Benedict Cumberbatch again, it's "like my frontal lobe is very disappointed in my cerebral cortex." She feels like she's letting herself down. Or maybe I'm just projecting.

Is it an affair of the mind? Another woman tells me she knows she's not doing anything wrong by having feelings for Benedict Cumberbatch—literally, she says, "I know I'm not doing anything wrong"—but still, she keeps it from her husband. She doesn't want to make him feel bad. She loves her husband! And how would you feel if you found out your wife knows exactly which minute to fast-forward to in *Doctor Strange* so that she lands, just perfectly, on that scene where Benedict Cumberbatch is wearing only a towel (00:43:30)?

"I wouldn't like it if *he* did it," someone else tells me. Actually, a lot of people tell me this, meaning they wouldn't like it if their husband had similar feelings for a celebrity, like, for example—and then they always say "Scarlett Johansson"—Scarlett Johansson. It's true, I wouldn't like that.

People without partners can feel bad too, of course. They

feel bad for what they're doing to Benedict Cumberbatch, objectifying him. "The idea of being in an art gallery, and looking at a piece of art, and turning around and seeing people taking photos of you, is really perverse," Benedict Cumberbatch has said. Just because someone looks like a piece of art doesn't mean you should treat them like one. Objectification turns people into things, and don't women know the cost of that all too well? Now you're letting down the whole of feminism. We look; we're sorry; we feel bad. Almost makes you wonder if it's worth it.

Why *do* you want to know what my husband thinks? I'm not getting you into trouble—I wanted to know too. And even though I obviously know the answer now, I still don't understand why it mattered to me so much. How can it, really, have anything to do with him? But also, it seems like it's entirely about him.

❤

IDLING ONLINE ONE DAY, I FIND A POST ASKING PEOPLE to fill in a survey about their experience of having a crush on a media figure. I click on it because, sure, I'll answer some more questions about what I'd like to do with Benedict Cumberbatch's dirty napkin. But this is a very different survey from the one about celebrity worship syndrome. It's not a mental health check; it's more like couples counseling. The couple in question is me and Benedict Cumberbatch.

Right up top, the survey asks you to name the media figure you've had romantic feelings for. It can be a fictional character or a real person. Then, from that point on, the survey becomes personalized. This is how I find myself contemplating the following: *In general, how satisfied were you with your relationship with Benedict Cumberbatch?* I chuckle, and select *Extremely satisfied.* You know it. The next question is *How well did your relationship with Benedict Cumberbatch meet your needs?* Hmm, this is getting a bit freaky, I think, and then I answer with the highest available option on the scale, number seven: *A great deal.* When I see that the next question is *How good was your relationship with Benedict Cumberbatch?* I can only reply with a question of my own. Okay, so who wrote this survey and why are they making it sound like I'm in a real relationship with Benedict Cumberbatch?

"Imaginary love is real," says Dr. Riva Tukachinsky Forster. She's an associate professor at Chapman University in California, specializing in media psychology. She's also the author of that survey. Dr. Tukachinsky Forster studies parasocial romantic relationships, which is the technical name for a crush on a media figure. She believes that these relationships, like between me and Benedict Cumberbatch, can generate feelings as meaningful and profound as reciprocated, unmediated relationships, like between me and my husband. Her survey questions aren't buying into a delusion; they're simply recognizing the existence of these feelings.

When we speak, Dr. Tukachinsky Forster begins by telling me, with raised eyebrow and a coy look, that she *fully* endorses Benedict Cumberbatch as a love object. And here I was, thinking I was finally speaking to someone outside the Cumberverse, but truly, it seems safer to assume that everyone is a Cumberbitch. Her first love, though, was Mac-Gyver, she says: the original one, played by Richard Dean Anderson. At school, she used to dream he would turn up and rescue her from the bullies.

She didn't give much thought to MacGyver after puberty. But then, decades later, she became a mother. "I was getting Netflix DVDs to get me through the nights of breastfeeding and colicky baby-burping," she remembers, and *MacGyver* was among them. At first, it was hard to watch the show because the acting isn't great and the production values are laughable now. "But then," Dr. Tukachinsky Forster says, "I just felt like, he's been there all this time." This experience sparked her research interest in parasocial romantic relationships. It's a "quest for self-understanding," she says.

"This same thing happened to me when I became a mother!" I tell her. "That's why I want to speak to you!"

"Yes, of course," she says, as if it's the most normal thing in the world. "There's a section on maternity in my book on parasocial romantic relationships," she adds, like it's a standard part of child-rearing. You have a baby, you feed the baby, you burp the baby, you fall in love with a man on the television. "It's an important way to renegotiate a new identity. I didn't experience it that way in real time, but now, in retrospect, when I hear other women speaking about it, I think maybe it was that for me as well," she says. "I definitely was lost, so it was a good thing." I feel like her quest for self-understanding is progressing at a faster pace than mine.

Dr. Tukachinsky Forster believes that while there definitely can be negative experiences associated with parasocial romantic relationships—just like there definitely are fans whose behavior is delusional or antisocial—for the most part, they're understudied, stigmatized, and normal. The term "parasocial relationship" has a pathological tilt to it, she says, because it was coined by psychiatrists in the 1950s. But you can be perfectly fulfilled in your real-life relationships, and totally satisfied with your romantic partner, and still seek out a parasocial romantic relationship; it doesn't have to reflect badly on your spouse. And, Dr. Tukachinsky Forster says, such relationships aren't usually a substitution or surrogate for low self-esteem or loneliness either, even though this is how parasocial romantic relationships were characterized—like a kind of security blanket—by research on "media uses and gratifications" in the 1970s and 1980s.

Maybe a celebrity crush is compensating for insecure real-world relationships for some people, Dr. Tukachinsky Forster says, but it's simply not the case for most people. "The numbers are not there. I can see it from study after study. However you measure it, there is no correlation between all the things we would expect to be a deficit that calls for a substitution relationship and having parasocial romantic relationships.

"What we do find consistently is that people who are more prone to forming strong real-life social bonds are also more likely to form strong *parasocial* bonds. Parasocial relationships are just an extension of our social relationships; the same mental models that organize our non-media-based relationships, they also organize our media relationships. We didn't evolve long enough with media around us to develop a different part of the brain to handle imaginary relationships and imaginary people. We're using the same infrastructure to handle both."

"So hang on," I say, "doesn't that mean I really *am* mind-cheating on my husband, then? If I'm storing him and Benedict Cumberbatch in the same part of my brain?" This, Dr. Tukachinsky Forster says, is a personal question, not one she can answer with empirical evidence. "But," I ask a little anxiously, "do you think these are the kinds of feelings one should keep to oneself?"

"A lot of women are comfortable telling their significant other about what they're going through, and it's taken okay. They tell me their husbands tease them about it, and it becomes a funny thing," she says. "But if you have internalized the negative social stigma that you're behaving in an immature way, then maybe you won't want your husband to know about it. Or, maybe you want to keep it to yourself, in a corner of your soul that's just for you. Or, perhaps your husband would be threatened by it, I don't know. My question to you would be, how would you feel if your significant other had similar feelings toward—"

"Scarlett Johansson," I say, preemptively.

"Yes, Scarlett Johansson? It's a personal thing."

❤

OUT OF ALL THE PEOPLE I ASK TO SPEAK WITH ME ABOUT their feelings for Benedict Cumberbatch, Linda is one of the very few who don't want to talk on the phone. She's seventy-four, and her husband is with her most of the time at their home in a rural area of the southern United States, so private phone calls aren't really possible. She emails me instead. Her typing is impeccable—she used to work in the software industry. I'm a bit worried about why Linda has to be so secretive, though. Is she *afraid* of what her husband will think? No, she writes back. She just wants to keep it to herself.

"I'm of the opinion that I'm not required to explain why I feel or think the way I do," she says. She found it hard to answer the questions I had emailed her, she says, for this exact reason. "I give what I can of my love, time, and support to my family and friends, but reserve the right to have a private, inner life." For over thirty years, her family and her work consumed her. "Most of the adult privacy I have had was in my own head." Later, she tells me that she and her husband decided long ago that "it doesn't matter where you get your appetite as long as you dine at home. And we don't necessarily share where we get our appetites."

Emma, the professor, says something similar to me when she answers my final question, about whether her husband knows that she writes fic. No, she says, it's private. "Some women write diaries, and I write fanfiction. It's only for me."

"But then your husband doesn't really, fully know you?" I ask.

"Sure," she says, "but you know what? I'm fine with that. I think the reason that he and I are so constantly stimulated, and pleased with our complicity, is that we still bring a lot of mystery to the relationship. Even after all these decades."

"You don't feel like there's any betrayal there when you write explicit love scenes?"

"Not at all," she says. "I think fantasies are free. He, no doubt, has an erotic imagination, stimulated by lots of people. It's none of my business."

The woman on the phone in her marital home—the one who wanted to remain so anonymous that I honestly can't think of how else to describe her—she says she keeps her thing for Benedict Cumberbatch on the down low because "people would start wondering questions I don't want them to wonder about—about my marriage and why my husband allows it. I know how people's brains work, so I keep quite a big moat around me. It's about a sense of being in control of who I am as an adult."

And then there's Jade. Years after that night at her house, when she didn't tell her husband I was there, I eventually ask her about it. We're at a weekday matinee screening of *The Courier*, starring Benedict Cumberbatch, enjoying our complimentary tea and carrot cake (which they apparently put on for the senior citizens who attend movies at this time). We are better friends now than we had been that night, thanks to the passage of time and the continual release of new Benedict Cumberbatch content. "Why didn't you want your husband to know about what we were doing?" I ask Jade.

"Because I didn't want him to ruin it," she says.

"Oh, I thought you were ashamed," I say.

"No," she says. "I didn't want to have to hear what he'd say."

Dr. Tukachinsky Forster is right: it's a personal thing. But I still can't work out why it matters so much to know what my husband thinks of all this.

❤

IT'S NOT NECESSARILY A BAD THING TO WONDER WHAT other people think, of course. It's considerate, empathetic. It's practically the definition of "feminine." There's a study about that: researchers asked American women to consider the messages they receive about how they're *supposed* to act, think, and feel, as women, and used their answers to develop a list of perceived "feminine norms."

Steel yourself, because here's the result, an inventory of how women are *supposed to be*: nice in relationships, thin, modest, domestic, caring for children, invested in romantic relationships, sexually faithful, and invested in our appearance.

Awesome list. Love it. I think "thin" is my favorite, because it doesn't pretend to be anything else. Just: thin! Another highlight is how many of these feminine attributes aren't even about women but about other people and how women make them feel. Taken together, caring *a lot* about how you make other people feel comprises a good chunk of what it supposedly means to be a woman.

It's pertinent to note that the original study was conducted over a decade ago, and with mostly straight cisgender women, but in further, more recent research on these norms, LGBTQIA+ women and gender-nonconforming people have endorsed them to the same extent as, or in some cases more than, straight cisgender women. It isn't surprising, really, that we all care so much about other people, especially men. You know the quote often attributed to Margaret Atwood: "Men are afraid that women will laugh at them. Women are afraid that men will kill them." Keeping one eye on how you make men feel might be necessary to your survival. But conversely, if you don't care *a lot* about how you make other people feel, it might end up seeming kind of wrong, transgressive. Shameful. Like you might want to keep that information to yourself.

❤

THE WHOLE SCARLETT JOHANSSON THING, THOUGH. I know I said I wouldn't like it if the situation with my husband were reversed, and that's true. But I don't think this reveals anything about me and Benedict Cumberbatch, or even anything about me and my husband. When a man ogles a woman, it's different from when a woman ogles a man. Just ask an ogled man, like Irish actor Aidan Turner—the shirtless, scything guy who put the "pole" in *Poldark*—who has said of his own objectification relative to that of women: "I'm a man. It's just not the same. It's a completely different world for me. I walk down the street, I don't ever feel scared. There are women who feel scared every day." Thanks, Aidan. Not just a pretty face—but a pretty face who knows all about the patriarchy. Hot. And, in my opinion, correct.

The act of *looking* isn't a bad thing, and there can be pleasure in being *looked at* too, but you're not doing it in a vacuum. It exists in a sociocultural, historical context. If Nathan, a heterosexual cisgender man, had a thing for Scarlett Johansson, it would refer, at least on first impression, to the context of sexist objectification of women by men, and the long tradition of a woman's worth being subsumed by, and limited to, that objectification. So no, I wouldn't be into it. If he had a thing for Aidan Turner, though, I'd be all for it.

It's interference, bringing up Scarlett Johansson. It's just more noise. A hypothetical counterexample that now—*gotcha!*—you have to factor in. And I know I just threw the word "patriarchy" out there with the kind of confidence that suggests I consider myself above engaging with bad-faith accusations of reverse sexism. But that's not the case. I have thought about—and felt bad about—the Scarlett Johansson question a lot. Of course I have! I assure you that I have considered how my thing for Benedict Cumberbatch affects other people *from every conceivable angle.* That's my go-to mode, always "in relation to," worrying about how I am making other people feel. It has to be that way. Because when you ask, "What does your husband think about all this?" what you really want to know is: "Have you performed all the necessary psychic labor to make sure your feelings are, you know, *okay* to share?" Have you done the work? If I had to take a guess, I'd say this is why that question feels like it matters so much. It's the same impulse that led me to Emma: we think we need a benediction, clearance to proceed, before we can feel good.

By buying into the question of what the husbands think, I'm doing something that comes so naturally to me, it feels essential: I am holding myself to account. Something makes me happy, or brings me pleasure, and I ask, how does this make me look? Nice? Thin? Modest? Domestic? Caring? Invested in my relationship? Sexually faithful? Like a good wife? I put everything through a pressure test, to see if it will hold up under public scrutiny, to see if it's *okay*. And if the pleasure doesn't consider the needs of other people, and if it doesn't attend to what other people require of me—if it's *just for me*—then it will fail. No wonder so many women prefer to confine their pleasures to the privacy of their inner life, or to their supportive online communities. It's the only way to escape the question of what your husband thinks about all this.

❤

THE FIRST TIME I SAW NATHAN, IT WAS OUT OF THE corner of my eye. It wasn't a stolen glance across a crowded room, it was literal side-eye. It happened while I was icing a cake in the tiny kitchen of my best friend's new apartment. Beth was having a housewarming party, and she had asked me to come before all the guests arrived because I was her best friend, and because I was good at things like icing cakes. I don't know why Nathan—a new friend of one of Beth's *other* friends—was there. Upon arriving, he gave Beth a blue glass vase with flowers already in it as a housewarming gift— totally over the top! Nathan then went straight to the kitchen to tell me that he knew a better technique for icing the cake. I did not take it well.

Beth still has that vase, and whenever she's using it, she always points it out to me. "Look, it's that *beautiful* vase Nathan got me!" It is a beautiful vase. He was also right about icing the cake. I hated him immediately and for a long time.

When I married him eight years later, Beth had a lot of good material for her wedding speech. She had set us up, after all. It was just a very long time before the side-eye became heart-eyes.

As these stories always tend to go, it was being too much alike that was behind both the hating and the loving. Nathan and I are very similar people. We like the same things, such as Beth, showing off, and being right. This manifested as mutual competitiveness in our twenties but mellowed into mutual admiration by our thirties, a destination we arrived at with the help of other relationships we had with other, not-so-similar people along the way. It turns out I'd rather be with someone in possession of big opinions on cake decoration than with someone who—can you imagine?—doesn't care about icing at all.

Because we like the same things, it wasn't that strange that Nathan sat on the couch and watched all those Benedict Cumberbatch movies and TV shows with me. We always watched things together—back when we used to catch planes, we would even coordinate pressing the play button on the little screens—and this was no different. And most of the things Benedict Cumberbatch has been in are the kind of things we both like to watch anyway, the kind of things favored by people who grew up on imported British TV.

What was strange, however, was Nathan's reaction on the night when I selected *Parade's End* as our next serving of Benedict Cumberbatch. It's a five-hour BBC miniseries based on the novels by Ford Madox Ford. "I've seen that already," Nathan said. "What? When?" I asked, taken aback, since we always watched everything together. How could he have watched *five hours* of TV without me? He shrugged. "Well, when you weren't here."

"What does your husband think about all this?" A question about Benedict Cumberbatch that I'm asked—all the time, by everyone, anywhere. Sitting at my desk at work. At school pickups, when I'm wearing a subtle but undeniably captivating Benedict Cumberbatch button on my cardigan. Pitching this book—which is not about Benedict Cumberbatch—to publishers.

"What does your husband think about all this?" A question about how motherhood nearly ruined me, which no one ever asks. A question about how I disappeared from myself, and from Nathan, and from the couch, going to bed at the same time as the children to get a head start on the night, which now ended, impossibly, at two a.m. A question about how we no longer seemed similar at all, but completely different, biologically opposed, two people on different schedules, having different experiences, who no longer saw the same TV shows, nor the world the same way. The emoji with the crosses for eyes.

Why don't you ask what my husband thought about *that*? Because a mother's trials aren't a matter for her husband, only her pleasures? But, you see, the pleasures weren't the problem. We'd been driven apart already, and it had nothing to do with Benedict Cumberbatch. And whether you want to know or not, I'll tell you what Nathan thought about that: it was terrible! It was a miserable time for us. And he'd have done anything to make it better.

"I'm happy to watch it again!" Nathan said, and he really was. *Parade's End* is so good you could watch it on loop forever, every time noticing something new about Benedict Cumberbatch's mouth. "The things he can do with his mouth are quite amazing," writes the *New Statesman* in their review; "it seems almost to inflate with emotion, sometimes with the result that he looks like an exotic fish." But Nathan didn't care about Benedict Cumberbatch's mouth. He was happy to watch *Parade's End* again because he was happy we were sitting on the couch, watching something—anything!— together. If he noticed Benedict Cumberbatch's recurring presence, night after night, it mattered less to him than mine.

So, yes, Nathan sat, uncomplaining, in front of that exotic fish tank for a long time. But everyone has their limits. Except, it turns out, me. When it came to multiple repeat viewings—that's right, I mean repeats of repeats—he had to put his foot down. The never-ending *Sherlock* was what did it in the end. It's unconscionable the number of times I expected him to watch that show, but I was helpless to stop! Benedict Cumberbatch's hair has never been better than as Sherlock Holmes, so what could I do? As a concession, I would let Nathan "choose" which *Sherlock* episode it would be (there were only ten episodes to choose from).

One night, I was making Nathan this great offer when he replied something along the lines of "Seriously? Again?"

And I said, "It's better than anything else on TV!" Which was certainly true, hairwise.

"C'mon!" Nathan said. "There's got to be something else."

I gasped and recoiled. There was not, at that point in my life, anything else. It was just Benedict Cumberbatch's hair. My (over)reaction confused Nathan, so then he said the words that still, to this day, make my pulse quicken and no doubt his too: "What? It's just a show!" Dun-dun-dun DUNNN.

Nathan was sitting on the couch readying the laptop for watching. I was standing up, tidying the kids' toys away. This was handy because I was able to fling bits of Duplo into a tub as percussive accompaniment to the finer points of my rage. That was the scene: a man who had no idea what he had just walked into, and a woman pacing and ranting, and also, tidying. I'm sure I don't need to tell you that this is a very dangerous combination.

I went *off*. That it's "just a show" is exactly the problem, I howled. How can a TV show have taken on such outsized significance in my life? Because there's nothing else to compete with it, that's why! What had my life become? I wailed. There was *nothing* that was my own. All I had was Benedict Cumberbatch!

I hated that Nathan got to go to work every day, I said, making his time valuable and mine expendable. I hated that

I had nothing to write about. I hated that I was always the one managing the children's relentless life admin. I hated that he never noticed when the vacuuming had to be done. I hated that his sense of self didn't appear to be in any way affected by parenthood, while I was experiencing a cosmic disturbance of such magnitude that I did not know who I was anymore. I mean, who was I? I'd been reduced to a pathetic teenager again! Nathan furrowed his brow but let the rant continue uninterrupted. And continue it did, on and on, down many paths that had nothing to do with TV shows. Eventually Nathan put the laptop away because it was clear we would not be watching anything.

I honestly can't remember all the things I said. I'm sure most of it was worth forgetting. I do recall a part where I offered a pretty convincing analysis of why I loved *Sherlock*. "It's because, unlike me, Sherlock Holmes gets to do whatever he wants!" I said. He doesn't have to be nice to people and has no responsibilities beyond maintaining his hairdo. He is completely above "the dull routine of existence!" A good theory. But it's one that hinges on me wanting *to be* Sherlock Holmes more than wanting *to do* him. Maybe this was true at the time, my love being more for the character than the person. Or maybe I thought it would be easier to explain it to Nathan this way, softening the blow, so to speak.

In any case, Nathan sat and listened to the whole thing. He did not bring up Scarlett Johansson. He did not bring up anything. At the end of it all, he nodded and said, "Well, this is good to know." I went to bed, exhausted. At least the house was tidy now. The next morning, Nathan got up early to make breakfast for the kids, saying I should use the time to write, in the spare room. "I think you actually *do* have something to write about," he suggested. He's always right. It's annoying. Then he bought a robot vacuum cleaner and called it Benedict Cumbervac.

And really, that's about all there is to say about what my husband thinks of all this. The answer to the question is less interesting than our need to ask it. Nathan buys me Benedict Cumberbatch stuff. He watches all the new TV shows and movies with Benedict Cumberbatch in them and talks about them with me for much longer than anyone else could bear. I save the repeat viewings for when he's out of the house. "Have fun with Benedict!" he'll shout on his way out the door. He made me a Benedict Cumberbatch cake for my birthday one year, cutting out a stencil of Benedict Cumberbatch's face and dusting icing sugar over a chocolate slab cake to make a dreamy white silhouette. Except while making it, he reached for the wrong jar and accidentally used cornstarch instead of icing sugar, so after singing "Happy Birthday" and blowing out the candles, we had to wipe Benedict Cumberbatch off the cake with a paper towel before we could eat it. You might think this was Nathan's way of sending a passive-aggressive message—"Not so dreamy now, my starchy friend!"—but I know that Nathan would never make a cake wrong on purpose.

If Nathan does find my behavior demeaning, he has never said so, despite all my prodding to try to get some good material out of him for this chapter. It would be a much better narrative climax if he had said, "It's either me or Cumberbatch!" and then our marriage fell apart. But he's not that guy.

The bottom line is this: Nathan saw that my thing with Benedict Cumberbatch was weirdly important to me; it offered me something that I obviously needed, and most importantly, it had nothing to do with him. He gave me something much better than his permission: an exemption from having to care what he thinks. He's *that* guy, the one man in the world who is more attractive to me than Benedict Cumberbatch.

And unlike me, Nathan has never shied away from telling anyone about my "thing." He doesn't see the problem with it, because he hasn't spent his whole life worrying *a lot* about how he's making other people feel. In fact, Nathan loves me loving Benedict Cumberbatch more purely and joyously than I have ever been able to love Benedict Cumberbatch myself, because he's not racked with guilt and shame over it all.

Also, good things really do come to those whose wives are obsessed with Benedict Cumberbatch. When boyfriends come up to Benedict Cumberbatch to say their girlfriends are obsessed with him, he shouldn't say he's sorry. He should say, "You're welcome." The eggplant emoji.

♥

IF NATHAN HAD REACTED DIFFERENTLY, IF WE WEREN'T so similar, what would that have changed? I don't know. I think for some women, it's not worth finding out what their husband thinks; women have been murdered for less. It's not just about husbands either, of course. It's everyone else too: your parents, your children, your boss, your neighbors. For what it's worth, among the people I have spoken to about Benedict Cumberbatch, those in relationships with women or nonbinary people all tell me their partners know about their proclivities and are fully in support.

When I ask Linda from Arkansas if she's really *choosing* to keep her inner life private, or whether the choice has been made for her, dictated by the judgments of others, she says maybe, but it's about self-protection. People conflate any kind of difference with abnormality and aberrance, she says, and that includes women who read erotic fanfiction. She doesn't want to be left "twisting in the wind," at the mercy of public opinion. It can turn on you in a heartbeat, she warns. It's a shame though, she adds, because she has a close relative who is gay, and she'd love her to know about fanfiction, "but I doubt that I'd ever tell her myself." Maybe, she continues, "I'll get my daughter to send her a copy of whatever you write."

I start getting up earlier and earlier to go into the spare room. Sometimes I write, sometimes I just waste my time looking at photos of Benedict Cumberbatch on the internet. As the sounds of the waking household begin to seep under the door, I stay in there just a bit longer. What a weird feeling it is, to know what I want, and to take it; even weirder, really, than finding myself in love with a celebrity.

chapter ten

this is not a chapter about *police academy*

"If I were to say what I was feeling and thinking,
no one would want to be with me."

When I was around six or seven years old, I was really into the *Police Academy* franchise. Why, you might ask, was a child that age even watching these films at all? The first movie in the series is rated R, and features, if I recall correctly, a sex worker performing fellatio on a police captain while he gives a speech. So yes, it's a good question! I think it was the perfect storm of eighties parenting (and I use that word *verrry* loosely), teenage siblings, and market saturation—there was a *Police Academy* movie released *every single year* from 1984 to 1989. How they made such quality films so quickly, we'll never know.

Understandably, this has been a source of lifelong amusement for my brother and sisters. *Police Academy* is a wacky foundational text for anyone, but it's particularly wacky that it's mine, because it's completely incongruous with everything else about me at that age. I was so wholesome! I was the archetypal little sister, all about Strawberry Shortcake and Narnia and pressed flowers and saving the whales. And there I was, my hair in plaits, wearing my pulled-up socks, coming home from school and sitting myself down in front of our wood-veneer TV, for some good old-fashioned T&A, *Police Academy*–style.

There was a boy in my class who also inexplicably loved *Police Academy*. I'm going to call him James to protect his anonymity, because if anyone understands the enduring negative consequences of people knowing about your childhood obsession with *Police Academy*, it's me. At lunchtime, James and I would meet in shady spots on the school oval, starting all our sentences with "What about the bit where Hightower . . ." or "How about when Mahoney . . ." We would marvel at Michael Winslow's vocal sound effects and do Bobcat Goldthwait impersonations. Probably, we wondered together why the patrons at the Blue Oyster were all men, in leather.

There came a point, however, when I started to feel self-conscious with James. I clocked that having a boy for a best friend wasn't the done thing for a girl. Whenever I saw James playing handball with the boys, I would feel embarrassed about our connection. I knew it was never going to work; despite our shared interest, he was one thing and I was another. I knew all about this because when I wasn't watching *Police Academy*, I was watching inappropriate John Hughes movies with my sisters. I had already learned that we all fit into a type, like the characters in *The Breakfast Club*. It's simply a matter of identifying which one, and then sticking with others like you. I leaned into the Barbies with the girls, and James no doubt leaned into handball, and we drifted apart.

He and I went to different high schools, but we lived in a small town, so throughout my adolescence I would see him at the shops or waiting at the train station. We always avoided eye contact and never said a word to each other. Teenage girls and teenage boys really are one thing and another. When I passed him, I would think about *Police Academy*, and burn with embarrassment at the memory of our misguided friendship, built on such a flimsy pretense. And that's how I've felt about the whole experience ever since. Sure, I can laugh about it, but the blazing mortification hasn't ever really died down. It's the feeling of having done the *wrong thing*.

Over the years, I have occasionally wheeled out the fun fact that I was obsessed with *Police Academy*, including once on a blog I kept with some friends as a way to stay in touch with one another. In a post about childhood memories, I wrote that James and I bonded because there was literally no one else in the Venn diagram crossover between *Police Academy* connoisseurs and actual infants. The blog, which was never really intended for public consumption, eventually fizzled and sat dormant on the internet for years, as these things do.

And then James found it. Here was a person I had not spoken to since primary school and with whom I had absolutely no connection in real life or on social media, and then his name popped up right there in the comments. Wild! And what do you think he said? "Dying! How embarrassing were we? Hightower FTW!"? Or how about "LOL, I finally figured out what they were up to at the Blue Oyster!"? Nope. He did not mention *Police Academy* at all.

"Some of my most vivid memories of growing up in Wentworth Falls relate to my childhood friendship with Tabitha," he began. "The impossibly steep climb from the primary school to her house on hot sunny afternoons, the luxury of a playground with swings right opposite her house, and her enormous and overly affectionate dog." (Oh, Ernie! He really was the best dog.) "Most of all," James continued, "I just remember that I enjoyed her peaceful company."

I sat back in my chair, a little stunned. It was hard to take it in, the idea that I existed in James's mind like this: a fully fleshed-out girl, belonging in the world. I had forgotten her completely. But he had somehow preserved the memory of our friendship for what it was, unrevised by embarrassment, or the need to make everything a punch line. He'd allowed us to have weird taste, to change and grow apart, all a normal part of childhood, without erasing anything about who we were at the time. And what had I done instead, with the memory of this lovely girl, and this genuine friendship?

I think it's easy to sacrifice your former self. In 2019, *Jezebel* writer Tracy Clark-Flory published a story called "*Jagged Little Pill* Is Actually Very Bad???" about revisiting the Alanis Morissette album, a favorite from her youth, and finding it wanting. Memorably, she decided that it was the equivalent of "Baby Shark" for "mid-'90s angsty tween girls." As you can imagine, and as may have been the intention of the article, there was a huge backlash. In *Variety*, Kay Hanley, the singer from the nineties band Letters to Cleo, published a scathing response.

"I don't fault anyone for outgrowing the music of their youth," Hanley writes, saying that it's fine if people don't like Alanis. "What pisses me off about the *Jezebel* piece is the arrogantly reductive re-framing of history and the baffling confidence with which the author is willing to invalidate and erase the opinions of her younger female self." Why does Alanis need to be "aggressively disowned," she writes, rather than "left to dissolve happily into the fabric of one's personal experience"? "Why not leave a space for that impact to maintain its resonance?" she asks about the things that once held meaning for us. "Why drag a sweet memory out into the town square and shoot it in the head?"

Because disavowing our past selves is part of the fabric of female experience too, isn't it? It's not that baffling. We shoot our memories in the head, but it's in self-defense, a preemptive strike against future denigration for loving the wrong thing, or loving it in the wrong way, or being the wrong kind of girl. We're not like that anymore; you can't hold that against us. We're always staying one step ahead, holding ourselves to account, acting our age, always on the outside looking in. You can't get hurt that way—which is good! But it's hard to cultivate a coherent sense of *who you are* when it's built on *how you seem*. The foundations are too shifting.

The pioneering feminist psychologist Carol Gilligan calls this process of holding ourselves at arm's length "dissociation." It's a split in consciousness, she says, which begins for girls in adolescence—or at least, that was the case for the adolescents she studied, belonging broadly to Generation X. In her book *The Birth of Pleasure*, Gilligan writes that before the teenage years, young girls can move easily, their voices free from "second thoughts and instant revision" (unless they have watched too many John Hughes movies before they can properly understand them). Then in adolescence, "girls often discover or fear that if they give voice to vital parts of themselves, their pleasure and their knowledge, they will endanger connection with others and also the world at large." You won't fit in. It's not the done thing. Ermahgerd.

Gilligan observed teenage girls in this state "beginning not to know what they knew." They give up the right to their own knowledge; they start to call their honest feelings "crazy." She quotes Iris, a seventeen-year-old girl from her study, as saying, "If I were to say what I was feeling and thinking, no one would want to be with me, my voice would be too loud."

Desire becomes overlaid with shame, and as a result, girls start to conceal their "vital, curious, pleasure-loving soul." We dissociate ourselves from her, erase her from our histories, because it's easier to make our way in the world that way. On some level, Gilligan says, we're aware of what we're sacrificing by dissociating from our desires, but this "awareness of complicity is so shameful that it often seems easier to justify it than to experience and question what has been sacrificed."

It's a clever but costly "psychic mechanism that allows survival in patriarchy," she says. And it's one we're taught. Gilligan remembers herself being twelve, and recalls "the sounds of my mother's voice and the voices of women teachers telling me what I needed to know, their voices often sounding as if they were speaking for someone other than themselves." I shuddered in recognition when I first read that: I am one of these women now. I see my teenage nieces transgressing all the supposedly inviolable rules we were taught as teens, about who is allowed to wear what and do what, and I think it's absolutely bloody marvelous, the literal best. And I also feel extremely worried about what people might say. "Someone other than myself" still seems to be in charge of my central processing unit.

The Birth of Pleasure is a strange book. It moves between Greek myth and psychological research and Anne Frank's diary as if they're one and the same. I'm not entirely sure about the scientific foundations for Gilligan's idea of dissociation. All I know is that at one point, Gilligan starts to remember the sound of her own unrevised voice of girlhood, "at once familiar and surprising," and then she has a dream where her "head spins around 180 degrees like an owl's," and I have never related more to anything in my life. That's how I felt when I read that message from James: utterly disoriented. This is me. This is not me. This is me. This is not me.

Maybe my owl is doing more like a 360-degree rotation, which was even freakier.

The thing with James and the blog comment happened years ago now. After my initial shock, I stopped thinking about it. And why would I want to? It was clear evidence, a witness statement, that once I actually was 4 REAL. Once, I didn't know about labels and what-kind-of-girl; I was happy just to be myself. My pleasures were inexplicable but they were expressed. If I thought about it too much, I'd have to tally the cost of her loss. So I shoved the memory of her back where she'd been, out of sight, like my sister's purple wig; like the old copies of my fanzine, stowed away in boxes within boxes, too hard to look at, especially through eyes half-closed from cringing. Or is it wincing? Embarrassment for who I was, or grief for her loss? It's difficult to tell. From the outside, it kind of looks the same.

❤

WHEN I WAS MOVING OUT OF HOME TO GO TO UNI, sorting my clothes into piles to either take with me into the next stage of my life or donate to the thrift store, I hesitated, for a moment, over my band T-shirts. I held up the (men's) U2 shirt I bought at their concert when I was fourteen. It was extremely large, of course. The young people today who think they're wearing retro, nineties-style clothes, couldn't possibly conceive of how many sizes up they'd need to go to replicate how we actually looked at the time. U2 was the first concert I ever went to. I had traveled to Sydney on the train by myself, and queued outside the stadium all day to secure a good spot near the front. The people next to me in the queue, a bunch of people in their early twenties, took me under their wing, shared their snacks with me, involved me in their chatter, and made me feel cool.

Looking at the T-shirt, I found myself horrified by this memory, now altered by being close to my twenties myself. What a total drag I must have been to those poor people! God, couldn't I see that they were just taking pity on a child with no friends? I shoved the shirt into the garbage bag destined for the thrift store. What a waste, when I could still be wearing it today as a floor-length nightie. Then I shoved all the other band T-shirts in the garbage bag too. I was growing up. From now on, my clothes would have stripes or spots—some chevrons, maybe?—but not men's faces.

I pulled down my posters, then carted armfuls of British music magazines to the recycling bin. I wouldn't be needing those anymore. "Being more mature than men, maybe women reach and discard their obsessions earlier," right? That's what my beloved book on pop fandom said about the gender disparity in music journalism. Women mature out of their pleasures. Men, on the other hand, get to hang on to theirs, turning them into lifelong passions, or even better, a career. Then they get to make cute jokes about how they never grew up. I tipped stack after stack of magazines into the bin, and watched them slide inside.

At uni, although I had well and truly given up on music writing, I still did some other writing here and there while I was waiting for blogs to be invented. One time for the student newspaper, I put my hand up to do a profile on the rock-star-cool Irish comedian Sean Hughes, who had once meant quite a lot to me, having appeared on the cover of *Select* magazine in 1993. During this era, he had been a pretty big celebrity in the UK as a regular panelist on the BBC2 music quiz *Never Mind the Buzzcocks*, but no one else at my Australian uni newspaper knew who he was. I guess because they hadn't spent their entire adolescence reading magazine articles about British TV shows they'd never even seen, three months after they'd aired. In any case, I got the assignment.

Sean was in Australia with his stand-up show but had also recently branched out from comedy to write a book, so in our interview I asked him about his dual identities as author and comedian. Great question! Just like a real journalist! He answered, talking about how he perceived the various parts of himself. Then, in return, he posed a question to me. "What about your makeup?" he asked.

My hand instinctively flung to my face in horror. My *makeup*? My makeup was a source of great anxiety for me, because while I knew I had to wear it because of my bad skin, I didn't know how to put it on properly. To find this out, I would have had to take myself to a cosmetics counter, which I couldn't do, because that would be like acknowledging I could look good, when *obviously*, it was not possible for me to look good. Sean Hughes must have noticed the beige boundary line connecting my face to my neck. Or maybe my furry upper lip, which darkened from the foundation it collected. Or maybe my nose! It's so big, nothing could hide its pothole-sized pores! I gawped, heart pounding, with no idea what to say.

Sean smiled, not unkindly, but who knows what he was thinking. He had a reputation for being difficult, but he was nice to me. I was sorry to hear he died a few years ago. "I mean, what *makes you up*?" he clarified, but not in the sense of clarifying lotion. "What is it that makes you who you are?" Yes, of course, I said, and then I don't know what else because I don't remember the parts of the story where I didn't humiliate myself.

But by misunderstanding Sean's question, I answered it perfectly. I mean, what kind of person would honestly think that a writer/comedian is asking them, completely unprompted, about *their face* during an interview? The kind of person who thinks it's a question worth asking. The kind of person who is so paranoid about how others perceive her, about whether she is being the right kind of girl in the right kind of way, that this paranoia actually *is* her makeup now.

❤

BENEDICT CUMBERBATCH CAME OUT OF NOWHERE, strange face, strange name. He tapped a message on my ribs in Morse code: *Who. Are. You?* Is it any wonder I couldn't reply?

It was hardly the fault of motherhood that I didn't know who I was. I'd already, long ago, lost my grip on the question itself, replacing it with *What should I be?* and *How do I look to you?* and *Excuse me, what options are available to me at this time?* My answer, such as it was, would only ever have been temporary anyway. Eve Ensler, of *The Vagina Monologues* fame, says that when we get caught up in fitting in and pleasing other people, it "makes everything murky." "We lose track of ourselves," she writes in her book for teens, *I Am an Emotional Creature.* "We make everything okay rather than real."

The "shattering" of motherhood didn't cause my identity crisis, it simply made obvious the extent to which I'd already lost track of who I was. My sense of self wasn't intact to begin with. It broke so easily, really, because it was a poorly envisioned, cobbled-together construction, nothing more than an accretion of missteps and corrections, layered one on top of the other—this is me; this is not me—like one of those papier-mâché craft projects you make using a balloon. Over the years, cracks would appear, and I'd paper over them, another yearning successfully withheld. Everything looks fine from the outside, but inside, it was never solid at all. It was all okay, rather than real.

Motherhood made a different impact, though, because this time, the crack started on the inside, impossible to ignore. It originated from that wrinkly balloon still somewhere inside me—my vital, curious, pleasure-loving soul—like it was filling with air again. It wasn't a shattering in the way I first thought, like a cup smashing on the kitchen floor. It was a bursting through, or a busting out from within: an obliteration of everything holding it down and smoothing it over.

The journalist Gail Sheehy, in her seminal book about life stages, *Passages*, says this experience is typical of "the predictable crises of adulthood." (The fact that something so novel to me was already "predictable" in 1976, when she wrote the book, is either very reassuring or extremely dispiriting; I don't know which.) Humans are not unlike lobsters, she writes. A lobster grows by developing hard, protective shells and then expanding from within them, sloughing off the confining outside layers as it does so. With "each passage from one stage of human growth to the next"—such as having a baby, a divorce, retirement, your kids leaving home, a death of a loved one, a serious illness—"we, too, must shed a protective structure." We need to grow bigger in order to meet the changes and challenges of our new life circumstance. But now the armor that previously kept us safe no longer fits. Our "cherished illusion of safety and comfortably familiar sense of self must be cast off, to allow for the greater expansion of our own distinctiveness."

It must be strange for a lobster to be without a shell. Scary, even. It's strange and scary for humans too, the state we find ourselves in after a big life change. Without our protective armor, Sheehy says, we are, like the lobster, "exposed and vulnerable, but also yeasty and embryonic again, capable of stretching in ways we hadn't known before." We find ourselves in possession of considerably more energy than we are used to, inhabiting a larger space than we are used to inhabiting. We start to know again what we once knew. We start to feel our old, forgotten feelings. This is the reverse of dissociation, Carol Gilligan says; it's association. We begin to recognize the extent to which we've been "held captive to a false story about ourselves."

All these middle-aged women, myself included, asking why it happened to us, why, seemingly out of nowhere, we fell in love with Benedict Cumberbatch, we are asking ourselves the wrong question. Instead, we should be wondering where he's been all this time. What took him so long to turn up? If this capacity to make ourselves so happy—just by being *into* something—has been inside us all along, what the hell have we been waiting for?

But it's true that Benedict Cumberbatch is ready only when you are. He's waiting for you to get naked, exposed. Also: yeasty? Sure, whatever you're into, Benedict. He wants you to free your pleasures from the constraints of shame, guilt, embarrassment, fear, and the approval of others. He wants you to know what you want. He wants you to feel good without also feeling bad.

I don't really regret throwing away my giant U2 T-shirt. Fashion has changed, and so has my taste. I think *Police Academy* is extremely problematic now, and I don't like U2's music anymore. But when I shoved that shirt into the garbage bag, I also did away with the whole idea of loving—anything—with that kind of fervor. It had seemed necessary, part and parcel of growing up, the putting away of childish things. I thought it had to be done. So I stopped loving like I used to. And this, I do regret.

♥

I PRINT OUT A PHOTO OF BENEDICT CUMBERBATCH—those eyes!—and stick him up on the wall above the desk in the spare room. And then I dig around in envelopes of old photos to find one of me at seven, my hair in long plaits, dressed in my school uniform, with white socks. I've got my arm around our big, shaggy dog Ernie. He does look enormous, but it's only because I'm so small. I stick the photo of this girl on the wall too, right next to Benedict Cumberbatch. They're good company, for me, but also for each other. That girl in the photo would not be surprised, at all, to find him there. She knows what it's like to love something. "I'm sorry," I say to her. "I'll make it up to you."

Benedict Cumberbatch looks down at me as I sit at the desk. *Who. Are. You?* he asks me with his eyes. He can say a lot with his eyes. But the answer's right there, for all to see. This is me. This is my makeup. It's who I've always been.

Hey, Benedict Cumberbatch. I'm ready.

part three

unencumbered

this is a chapter about girl stories

"When we look at a girl story, most of us go a tiny bit stupid."

Coming out as a Cumberbitch is easy. Since the inside of me is almost entirely Benedict Cumberbatch, it's simply a matter of drip-feeding it to the outside. I start by casually dropping Benedict Cumberbatch into conversation, at a rate of one mention per every five hundred times I think of him. Then I reply to people's text messages with Benedict Cumberbatch GIFs, deploying a mere fraction of the images of him saved on my phone. I stick up more photos of him in the spare room—then answer the questions from our guests about the man whose many faces have been staring at them all night.

Nathan does a lot of the legwork for me. He buys me wearable Benedict Cumberbatches, so now everyone can see my insides on my outside. It starts with a wooden brooch, laser-cut into the shape of Benedict Cumberbatch's silhouette, which I pin on my coat. The Cumberbitch is now available. At the farmer's market, the young woman at the mushroom stall points to the brooch and says, knowingly, "Hey, nice!" My favorite potato seller pauses before releasing my bag of Désirées from the grip of her fingerless gloves. She squints, and asks, "Who's that?"

"It's Benedict Cumberbatch!" I say.

"Ooh, I liked him on *Graham Norton*," she says, a sentence I will go on to hear from women my mother's age, every day, for the rest of my life.

In my office at the university, I start the process with a Benedict Cumberbatch calendar, because that's office-y. Some of the photos could be called alluring, though, with a top button undone here and there, so I'm a bit hesitant. It's the Scarlett Johansson thing. Then, during the delightful month of February—a stubbly Benedict Cumberbatch staring straight down the lens, so hot you wish it were a leap year—a professor from the faculty executive committee comes by. He passes my desk, stops, walks backward, and points at the calendar. I gulp. "*This* is Benedict Cumberbatch," he says, like David Attenborough identifying a fascinating species in the wild. I nod. Then, with an astonished shake of his head, he says, "My daughter *loves* this man." And he's off on his way, presumably to make more field observations about great British actors around campus. I take this as license to go to Cumbertown.

After all my carrying-on about how embarrassing and inappropriate everyone will say it is, I discover that, actually, most people run with it. I guess if they're talking about how embarrassing and inappropriate it is, they do so behind my back, which is nice of them. Perhaps people are just grateful to have something to talk to me about. God knows, when you're crammed into the office kitchen with your colleague whose name you've forgotten, a ready-made conversation starter is a gift you're happy to receive. "So you really like Benedict Cumberbatch, huh?" they say. Or frequently: "Big *Doctor Who* fan, are you?" (He is not in *Doctor Who*.)

But there are also a lot of questions about *why* I like Benedict Cumberbatch, or how such a thing could even be possible. Oh, and, of course, what my husband thinks about all this. A lot of people go out of their way to tell me that they just don't *get it*. I tell them to watch out because once, there was a time *I* also did not get it, and now look at me. The "truth about getting older is that there are fewer and fewer things to make fun of until finally there is nothing you are sure you will never be." That's a line from Jenny Offill's novel *Dept. of Speculation* that I now know by heart.

There's also a certain kind of person (jokes, it's always a guy) who sees me liking Benedict Cumberbatch and needs to tell me that they, in fact, *do* get it. It's *me* who doesn't get it. The IT support person tending to a problem with my work computer looks around my desk and says, "You do realize you don't actually *know* this dude?" Benedict Cumberbatch is an actor, you see, so he's pretending to be the kind of person that an idiot like myself would be stupid enough to fall in love with. Then the IT guy asks me to type in my computer password, and I hit the keys with more conviction than I ever have before in my life: *B3n3d1ct_4_eva!*

My best friend, Beth, tells me *her* best friend Brené Brown says you should keep a list in your purse of the people whose opinions matter to you. It's a handy reminder: you needn't worry about anybody else. My purse, which Nathan bought me, is patterned with a collage of Benedict Cumberbatch faces, so I don't need such a list. Cashiers who say "I love your purse!" are the only people worth listening to.

It's okay for people to like different things, I find myself saying, over and over again, to friends, and strangers, and IT guys. We all have different interests. Beth taught me this lesson too, years ago, when she developed another important list (she loves lists), this one being her "list of interests." She came up with this concept after she got tired of people asking her if she was going to renovate her house. She worked out the best way to shut down these conversations was simply to say: "Renovation is not on my list of interests." It wasn't figurative. She actually created a list of interests so "home renovation" could, specifically, not be on it. I told my sister Amber about this, and later she reported she was so inspired, she tried to construct her own list of interests, but wrote "gardening" and then had a minor breakdown because she couldn't think of anything else. Also, she doesn't even like gardening.

(What is on *your* list of interests? This is in parentheses so you can ignore it if you want to. I don't want another breakdown on my hands.) No, I've changed my mind; I want to know: What is on your list of interests?

We all have different interests; we all like different things. It's a statement of fact, and it's also an effective strategic defense. I will not be taking any more questions at this time. But it's not just about "different things," is it? Some of us like normal things, and some of us like weird things.

Just across from where I sit at work, there's the office of a very lovely colleague who supports some kind of football team called the Dragons. I know this because I've seen his Dragons mug, his Dragons glass, his Dragons poster, his Dragons flag, and his Dragons tattoo. I also receive his emails about the office football pool, in which, I imagine, he chooses Dragons Dragons Dragons as the winners in every game. He loves the Dragons as much as, if not more than, I love Benedict Cumberbatch. This is, of course, fine, because it's okay for people to like different things. But I do not think this is something he ever has to say.

When it comes to sport, intense passion—the kind that inspires you to get tattooed—is so *normal* that no one is going to question my colleague about it. I don't think people even see that his desk and my desk are of a kind. No one is going to ask him, "Can you explain to me this whole *Dragons* thing?" Instead, they'll ask, "How about that game?" And fair enough! Sport is so embedded into our lives that it gets its own little bit on the news every night. It would be extremely unrealistic if I expected Benedict Cumberbatch to occupy the same position in our culture as football (but what a world that would be). So I happily accept my fate as someone in a minority, whose thing is always going to be, relatively speaking, not normal, and therefore weird.

Who cares anyway! Once I worked out how to love loving Benedict Cumberbatch, it felt so good—you would not *believe* how good!—that I didn't mind if it made me the biggest weirdo in the world. I was so happy—you would not *believe* how happy!—that I would choose being a Cumberbitch over being normal any day, and every day. And I did.

This should be the end of the book, right? *How I Learned to Stop Worrying and Love What I Love.* Sounds like a good book! But if mountain climbing is on your list of interests, I think this is what you'd call a false summit. Because then I found out about the female birds, and I saw how easy it is to think you know all there is to know, especially if it's a girl story.

❤

ALTHOUGH IT MIGHT SOUND LIKE ALL I DO AT WORK IS decorate my desk with pictures of Benedict Cumberbatch, I do have a job. It's still the same one I mentioned before, at the university, writing stories about science research. As part of my working day, I get to interview amazing scientists, many of whom are at the top of their field. I read their research papers, arrange to meet them in campus coffee shops, and then ask them to explain their research to me. I drink a lot of coffee and, because I'm not one of the nation's preeminent scientific minds, between sips I get to say to these extraordinarily impressive people, "Sorry, you're going to have to explain that again" and "I'm afraid I'm still not quite getting it." I like to think of it as a humbling experience, you know?

One day at work, I come across a news clipping about Professor Naomi Langmore, an evolutionary and behavioral biologist who is researching the songs of female birds. And when I say "researching," it's more like she's "proving the existence of." She's been doing this—proving that female birds sing—for over ten years. *Hmm*, I think. This seems like a very long time to spend on something that surely can be answered by simply ticking a yes/no box under the question "Do female birds sing?" It sounds kind of odd, but I'm sure this is just another case of me not getting it.

"No, it's exactly how it sounds," Professor Langmore tells me over coffee. By the end of our conversation, though, I think it might be worse than it sounds, because it's not just about birds.

As a birdwatcher, Professor Langmore has always known that female birds sing. Right here in Canberra, if you're not too busy looking at the big owl, it's easy to see a singing female magpie or singing female fairy wren, maybe even in your own garden. But, as Professor Langmore would discover, seeing something with your own eyes is not always enough.

She tells me it all started right at the beginning of her academic career, when she was in France doing research for her PhD. She was in the field with her supervisor, observing alpine accentors, a species of bird in which both the males and females sing. "Look!" her supervisor exclaimed, indicating the birds before them. "The females are singing! That's so *weird*!" This is when it dawned on Professor Langmore that people think this completely normal bird behavior is *weird* when the females do it.

The literal, textbook definition of birdsong is that it's a male vocalization, Professor Langmore tells me. In the extremely rare instances when female birdsong has been acknowledged, it is as a "hormonal aberration" or a "nonadaptive by-product of male song." So Professor Langmore decides to correct this and publishes a paper proving that the female alpine accentor sings.

"The reaction was resistance," she remembers. People were happy to accept—okay, *fine*—that the female alpine accentor sings, but they weren't prepared to accept that it's not *weird*. "They would say, 'This is a really unusual species with a polyandrous breeding system and yes, in this particular species you get song.'" Just because you find one singing female doesn't mean female birdsong is normal. Only male birdsong is normal.

So Professor Langmore sets out to prove that other female birds sing too. And she does. With a team of (women) colleagues from around the world, she publishes a phylogenetic analysis to demonstrate that the majority of female songbirds sing: 71 percent of all species, in fact. But five years later, the finding still hasn't really caught on. Just last week at a journal meeting, she had to correct someone who said only male birds sing. The idea is so entrenched, she says, that even people who have read her papers, and even people who have seen female birds sing, struggle to change their perspective.

♥

"WHEN WE LOOK AT A GIRL STORY, MOST OF US GO A tiny bit stupid," writes the critic Lili Loofbourow in her *Virginia Quarterly Review* essay "The Male Glance." It's an essay about how we perceive art and culture created by and/or for women, and I can't stop thinking about it during my conversation with Professor Langmore. We "don't expect female texts to have universal things to say," Loofbourow writes, so we dismiss them outright, without any real consideration. We only glance at them, and we think that's enough to get all the info we need: they're just girl stories.

"The male glance is how comedies about women become chick flicks," Loofbourow explains. "It's how discussions of serious movies with female protagonists consign them to the unappealing stable of 'strong female characters.' It's how soap operas and reality television become synonymous with trash." It's why the taste-making music website Pitchfork didn't lower itself to review Taylor Swift's *1989* when it came out—waiting instead until Ryan Adams released a cover version of the exact same album.

Limited by our "generic expectations," we believe we know all there is to know about girl stories, so we refuse to even *try* to find out if we're wrong, if there might be more to them than we think. It's an easy, quick diagnosis, allowing us "to omnisciently not-attend, to reject without taking the trouble of analytical labor because our intuition is so searingly accurate it doesn't require it." (It's an incredible essay.)

If we happen to recognize that a girl story *does* have something to say, we tend to assume that "the effects these female texts produce are small, or imperfectly controlled, or, even worse, accidental." Just that one bird. We are blind, she says, "to female intentionality."

"Our starting assumption, to correct for our smug inattention throughout history," she suggests, "ought to be that there is likely quite a bit more to the female text than we initially see." Look for it, Loofbourow urges, and if you find something, point it out. "And we will be better for seeing as obvious and inevitable something that previously—absent the instructions—we simply couldn't perceive."

❤

PROFESSOR LANGMORE HAS NOW FORMED A WORKING group of biologists, all women, to advocate for sex-inclusive research. "The only way to spread the message is to keep talking about it," she says. I ask why the biologists are all women, and she says that's just who's been interested in taking part. They're now studying the *purpose* of this (common, normal) female song. She knows it's certainly not functionless, nor an aberration: "Females sing for all sorts of reasons—just like males." She says she's proud of their work. They're "doing the right thing by the female bird."

She asks if I have any questions, and I say no. It's all perfectly clear; I get it. I thank Professor Langmore for her time and tell her I'll send her the story when it's done. I pay for our coffees and walk across campus to my office.

It's funny how we decide what's normal and what's weird. It's not always to do with the *what* but rather the *who*. Two birdies can be doing the exact same thing, both singing, but only one of them is worth listening to.

My manager asks how the interview went, and I say, distractedly, "Good, good." It hasn't happened yet, but in the future, my manager will cross-stitch me a Benedict Cumberbatch portrait, and it will become the centerpiece of my shrine. What's happening now, though, is I'm looking at my desk, then I'm looking over at Dragons HQ, and back again.

Do I get it? Between me and my Dragons-loving colleague, one of us is a special case, and the other one is the default norm. I thought this was because of *what* we loved, and the relative popularity of the object of our affection, but maybe this was a bum steer. If you look instead at what we're *doing*, isn't it, in fact, the same thing? Aren't we both singing? And why am I saying "singing," to be metaphorically like the birds? There's no need for metaphors—we're literally doing the same thing, fanning over what we love. Put us in the football stadium, at a red-carpet premiere, and we're both screaming.

What *is* it we're doing? We're letting the soft animal of our body love what it loves. Is it our hobby? Our obsession? I never did work out what word to use, and I think that has cost me a lot of time. I got hung up on *what* I loved and could never really see beyond that. My thing, my jam, my pleasure, a fixation, a fascination, a cathexis, something on my list of interests. It's any and all of those things, but it's also something more. It's not just about what we love but how that love figures in our lives, and how it makes us feel. If you start thinking about it in this way, at the level of function, it's easier to see the commonality between football and Benedict Cumberbatch. And fanzines. Ikebana too. Or horse-riding, gardening, *Star Trek*, fanfiction, *Police Academy*, Leonard Cohen, birdwatching.

"The assignment of your time according to whatever the fuck you feel like," Emma called it. Eve Rodsky, in her book *Fair Play*, calls it "unicorn space": the "active pursuit of what makes you uniquely you." Her book is about how to balance the burden of invisible labor, and protecting your unicorn space, she says, is a nonnegotiable part of the process. Brigid Schulte, the author of *Overwhelmed*, calls it, simply, "play."

I wonder, did you write that list of interests? Is there anything on there that could be categorized as play—something that serves no purpose other than fun?

In *Overwhelmed*, Schulte quotes Stuart Brown, a psychiatrist and the founder of the National Institute for Play, who says that sport, whether watching it or participating in it, is an easy way to maintain at least some semblance of play in your life. He notes that it's predominantly men who are able to do this. For women, Schulte says, "there has never been a history or a culture of leisure or play," and after childhood, women "tend to lose play entirely." "There's just this huge sense of loss," Stuart Brown tells her. "But when you don't make that time a priority, there are huge consequences, emotionally, spiritually, and physically. Most all of us have a play nature and it's within our capacity to get it back." An easy way to make something a priority is to make it "normal." When something is assumed to be normal, a natural and necessary part of life, we're more inclined to defend it.

People of all genders love sports, of course, and can take advantage of this play space already sanctified by men, either by watching it or by participating in it. But even in sports, so rare is the sight of women freely having fun that when it does happen, it's a novel experience. Abby Wambach, the former star forward in the American women's soccer team, talks about this on an episode of the podcast hosted by her wife, Glennon Doyle. Wambach says people tell her all the time they're surprised by *just how much* they love to watch the women's soccer team in action. For women, Wambach believes, it's because they're experiencing a "great, deep learning about what could be." They're seeing what can happen if we embrace women's potential for play. We're conditioned to believe women *don't know how* to have fun, Wambach says, which is not true; it's just that most women "never have been given the chance or taken the opportunity to have fun." We're not used to seeing it.

Generally speaking, men have done a much better job—a phenomenal job, really—of protecting play as part of their lives, and generally speaking, a much worse job of welcoming other genders to share those spaces with them. Social trends researcher Rebecca Huntley says Australian men, despite being more likely to work longer hours in paid work, can, "for some reason," find more time than women to spend on recreation and leisure, every single day. I know men who take all-day fishing trips, and half-day bike rides, and overnight excursions to collectors' fairs. My friend Tristan surfs in summer and skis in winter. Nathan plays tabletop games with a group of guys every Monday evening. My friend Jimmy leaps up at the first sign of lightning to take photographs of storms, any time of day or night. My dad has dedicated an entire room in his house to his hi-fi system. My friend Brett has a cabinet full of *Star Wars* figures. Our neighbor has a yard full of cars he's taking apart, or maybe putting back together. I don't think any of them feel bad about it, nor should they.

Just yesterday, I took my son, Teddy, to the slot-car shop in Canberra's light-industrial district, where he stood alongside adult men as they raced little toy cars around a track. One of the men had driven to the shop in his replica Cobra roadster, now parked out front. "That looks like an expensive hobby," Teddy said as we walked in. While hanging around the shop, I read a flyer about an upcoming eight-hour tournament, the toy car version of the real-life Bathurst motor race. The man who works there said it's a competition for teams, but one year, he proudly tells me, he put in a six-hour stint by himself, just him and the little toy racing car. Like I said: a *phenomenal* job.

I know you don't have six hours available to do whatever you want, just playing, having fun, but imagine for a minute there's a flyer on a wall somewhere that could make it so. Can you see yourself in that picture?

I look at my desk. I am happy enough to be a full-grown fangirl, subverting the narrative of age-appropriateness and how women are supposed to be. I've done the necessary work to be out and proud about it. I know all the best lines to defend myself when the need arises. But I'm not that one weird, singing female alpine accentor, doing things a bit differently. That's just not how the story goes. She's not a radical bird, demanding you accept her for how she is. She was never doing anything different, nor singing "despite" or "even though" anything. She only looked like a special case because of our failure to accept that female birds sing, for all kinds of reasons, just like the males—and they always have.

Everyone likes different things, I say, to encourage acceptance of my weird thing, but that only emphasizes my outlier status. Instead, it should be: *everyone* likes different things. We *all* have the same capacity for fun. It's just that it only looks normal when some of us do it. For the rest of us, it's so normal *not* to that I think we've forgotten what we're even capable of.

❤

I AM NOT THE ONLY ONE IN MY FAMILY WITH A PASSION. Teddy practically exited the womb with one: things on wheels. I'm surprised he didn't come out like that, motoring on through. He learned to talk out of sheer frustration at our inadequate vehicular terminology. "Digger," I'd say, pointing, as I pushed his stroller along our street. "No—*backhoe!*" he'd snap back, the tiniest, most adorable mansplainer. And so I learned the difference between a dump truck and a flatbed truck, a front loader and a bulldozer. Garbage trucks would toot their horns for us; a man once let him sit in the driver's seat of his Bobcat; construction site workers would tilt their cement mixers to give him the best view. "Concrete mixer," Teddy would correct me.

Soon he focused his passion only on trains, but with twice the intensity of before. Now I knew the difference between the Santa Fe and the Flying Scotsman, the Rocket and the Mallard. I could name you all the *Thomas the Tank Engine* characters, as well as tell you what a tank engine is. Our carpet was crisscrossed with networks of wooden train tracks and little bridges to trip you up. Canberra is not exactly train-free, but it is extremely train-poor, and Nathan and I felt guilty about this, like we were forcing Teddy to live in the wrong habitat, a bit like we'd bought a pet dog whose coat wasn't suited to the climate. We did everything we could to assuage our guilt. I have ridden on a lot of miniature trains.

Now, Teddy is all about cars, specifically supercars. As I would discover, these are very expensive, very fast cars that look cool. When we all go to the library, he immediately peels off to the adults' nonfiction section to get car books emblazoned with the logos for *Top Gear* and *GQ*. He watches YouTube videos hosted by an Australian woman who calls herself Supercar Blondie. "Are you sure the SafeSearch is on?" I ask, nervously. Supercars are even rarer in Canberra than trains, so Teddy wrote in his best handwriting to the Lamborghini showroom in Sydney, saying how he'd never seen a Lamborghini because, tragically, his parents birthed him in Canberra. "From Teddy (age 8)." They replied with a Lamborghini cap and an invitation to visit the showroom, and so we drove all morning in our dented Camry to get there, and he wore the cap and everyone was thrilled.

No one questions how the whole thing started or why it persists, even though his parents' interests could be summarized as things *not* on wheels. "Boys will be boys!" and "Boys and their toys!" are comments we hear a lot. I hate these expressions, but I have to admit they're difficult to outright reject. His interests seem so innate, that they're something he just has to do, like a tadpole getting legs, to set him up for the rest of his life as a vehicle-loving frog.

I don't know if he will carry these passions into adulthood, but if he wants to, then he can. At one model train exhibition, during the train years, he looked around at all the old men, standing proudly in their engine driver's caps, commanding their miniature displays and fielding questions about gauge widths, and observed, wistfully, "You can love trains *forever*."

Teddy's little sister, Dulcie, has a passion too. She loves girls. She loves being a girl, and she loves all other girls, and she loves just the idea of girls: how they look, what they like, and what they do. From before she could walk, when she very cutely shuffled along on her bottom instead of crawling, she was fascinated by girls' clothes, the frillier the better. She would choose her own outfits and want to wear them all at the same time, layered over the top of one another, so that she resembled a shuffling little laundry pile.

When she became a toddler, she would stand in front of the mirror and make the motion of tucking her hair behind her ear, all for show, because her fine wisps weren't even long enough to reach. Neither was my hair, so it's not a gesture she learned from me. She used pen lids to mime putting on lipstick and painted her nails with markers. Meanwhile, my morning routine is to walk into the bathroom, pick up my tweezers, look in the mirror, say "I don't have time for this," and then walk out.

Now Dulcie is six years old and nothing has changed. She tells me she's going to move in with her best girl friend and they will both have babies and these babies will both be girls. If you play Guess Who? with her, she'll reject Peter, Bill, and Charles, fishing around in the box until she gets Maria, Claire, or—the best—Anita, with her pigtails tied with pink ribbons. Her brother gets frustrated, telling her that's not how the game works, but for Dulcie it is. It's about gazing lovingly upon her special, chosen girl.

She likes pink things, sparkly things, rainbow things, princess dress-ups, high heels, unicorns, fairies, babies, brides, butterflies, bunnies, Elsa, Mulan, Moana. She knows, just from their spines, which library books have been written to meet her particular demographic: the ones about mermaids and cats with big eyelashes, the ones with metallic embossing and glitter gritted onto the cover. She'll prize them from the shelf, and I'll groan, "Please, no, not that one," shove it back, and proffer a book about pirate dogs instead. I'll buy her a NASA T-shirt that will remain unworn while she continues to go about every day in sequins and tulle. I'll roll my eyes and cringe and despair with the other school moms over how, even here in the woke inner north of Canberra, even with our progressive parenting, our daughters have fallen for the type-casting of prescribed femininity.

"I don't encourage her!" and "She doesn't get it from me!" we say, loudly, from within our T-shirts declaring *This is what a feminist looks like* and *Girls just wanna have fundamental rights*. We talk about how we used to have a ban on the Disney princess movies but soon realized it was a lost cause. Our girls somehow knew everything about them anyway. Rapunzel has a purple dress, Cinderella's is blue. Dulcie tells me about a girl in her class called Taylor, "just like the song."

"You mean like Taylor Swift?" I ask.

"No," she says, "like the *Beauty and the Beast* song." She's never seen that movie, but nevertheless, she breaks into tune: "Taylor's old as time . . ." Isn't it just? I sigh with the other moms and say what a shame it is that the marketing has gotten to our girls so early, making victims of our poor daughters. There's always the hopeful coda to these conversations, though, that this phase won't last forever.

"She doesn't get it from me!" I say, but actually, I'm teaching Dulcie exactly what she needs to know. There are no such things as "girl toys" and "boy toys," but when a girl plays, it's somehow different. A boy does what he does because he has a passion, he follows his heart. It's a worthy pursuit, with inherent, universal, and lasting value, so we'd better support and protect it. When a girl does what she does, it's merely the by-product of outside forces. She's being manipulated into having inauthentic, disposable feelings for something with dubious appeal. Boys can enjoy play for a lifetime; girls are expected to mature out of it. It passes, just like their fads.

With one cursory glance, I dismiss what Dulcie likes and, along with it, the very notion that her own agency might have played a part in why she likes it. I am blind to her intentionality. I'm not *really* looking at what she's doing, and I'm not *really* listening to her, because I don't expect to find anything in this girl story worthy of my attention.

"I don't encourage her!" I say, and that's exactly the problem. I think I'm somehow outsmarting the gender trap by teaching Dulcie to resist its limiting confines; girls can be— *kapow!*—whomever they want to be. But what I'm really doing is shutting down her ability to assign her time however she wants. I'm teaching her that when you're a girl who really loves a thing, it's never just about you and your thing. I'm closing off her—literal!—unicorn space, where she can learn to be herself. "For centuries we have been letting men be men on account of their instincts and we've been doing the opposite to women," the writer Lisa Taddeo observes in the *Guardian*, "telling each other to fasten a corset around our instincts, bottle it all up, refrigerate it, drink red wine through a straw so as not to stain the lips."

When friends and family are buying Teddy and Dulcie presents, they'll say to me, "I know I can get Teddy anything to do with cars, but what does Dulcie want?" Dulcie wants high heels. Dulcie wants lipstick. Dulcie wants a handbag. Get her some pencils, I say. And just like that, I rip up *not only* her list of interests but the very idea that she's capable of having one. Then, one day in the future, someone will ask her what she's into, and she will be shocked to find that she doesn't even know.

❤

SOME THINGS THAT SEEM OBVIOUS STILL NEED TO BE proven over and over again. Female birds sing. Women play. We are capable of having fun. And when we do, it's because we want to—the same as anyone else.

"We're so past that dumb outdated narrative of 'Oh, these people are girls, so they don't know what they're talking about,'" Harry Styles tells *Rolling Stone* on the subject of his "fervent female fandom." "They're the ones who *know* what they're talking about. They're the people who listen obsessively. They fucking own this shit. They're running it." I think of the girl in her bedroom, listening obsessively to her Britpop records, and I think of all the girls at the concerts too. We had so much love to give, but it wasn't worth anything coming from *us*. And look, here in *Rolling Stone*, it says it doesn't have to be that way anymore.

We've moved on. I grew up in what feels like not only another time but another universe, and it shows. Cherie, a twenty-two-year-old *Sherlock* fan from Sydney, tells me the story of how a male colleague once complimented her by saying, "You're not like the other girls"— a sentence I would have killed to hear when I was twenty-two. But not Cherie, not now. "Don't say that. That's an insult," she replies to him. "I am actually very fond of the other girls, and what's wrong with that?" They own this shit.

Before Cherie was a *Sherlock* fan, she was a fan of One Direction, and before that, she loved Harry Potter. Her enthusiasms change, but she has no intention of ever growing out of fandom. "There's no age limit on liking things," she says, "and there's no age limit on human connection—for men, or for women, or for anyone." Yep, it's pretty straightforward. My story must seem so boring to her, and that's the correct take. It *should* be boring.

If I want to do the right thing by the girls—by *my* girl—I need to own this shit too. I don't want to drag anyone down with a dumb outdated narrative, one where it's somehow exceptional to be—*gasp!*—a woman having fun. I don't want to make myself into a curious object of interest. I shouldn't be asking for anyone's acceptance even though they don't get it, or despite how weird it is, or putting in any effort to convince them it's *okay*. I need to be more like the man in the slot-car shop. I need to be more like Cherie. I need to recast myself in this story as someone who is doing what she wants, because she's just as entitled to it as anyone else. And who should have started a lot sooner.

"My feelings are my own. I want to own those feelings," says Susan, a former Beatlemaniac interviewed by music journalist Hannah Ewens for her book *Fangirls*. Susan would scream for hours at Beatles concerts. The media dismissed it as "learned behavior," but she knows it wasn't. This was early in the Beatles' career, when their fans were mostly female, and also actual maniacs. Later, of course, their fanbase would be co-opted by serious male music aficionados whose feelings were never called into question.

"I behaved the way I did because I wanted to," Susan says now, age sixty-eight. Imagine having to say that! As if screaming isn't something that other people do, and have done at football matches every weekend since Beatlemania. But apparently we have to keep saying it. All that screaming was a huge energy release, Susan says. It felt like floating. "Let it go, enjoy it," she urges. "It's good for you." Take it. It's yours.

chapter twelve

this is a chapter about doors

"It really feels like, *oh*, you just never know what's possible."

A book like this, should it tell you what to do? It seems pretty presumptuous. You might be much happier than me; you might already know all this. I don't want to tell you what to do. But also, I'm *desperate* for you to know that it's worth it. Finding your thing, I mean. Feeling a spark of something, and instead of instinctively dousing it, fanning the flames.

It feels good. It feels good in a way that's hard to get across because the alternative, not having a thing, doesn't necessarily feel bad, just normal. Although, there *was* that story I heard from a woman in my Facebook mothers' group, whose child brought home some schoolwork she'd done about her family. "My dad's hobby is brewing beer," the child had written. "My mum's hobby is the washing-up." I bet that felt bad. Also, there was that time I was running late to get Dulcie from preschool, and I grabbed her brother's hand and told him we better hustle as we jogged down the street. He looked up at me, wide-eyed with shock. "Mum!" he said. "You can *run*?!" That was quite funny, actually. I laughed. And then, my stomach sank. When did I become so small?

I'm bigger now, enlarged. Which is weird, because you'd think being that woman who loves Benedict Cumberbatch is pretty limiting as far as personal brands go, but it's not. In *Passages*—the book with the lobsters—Gail Sheehy writes that the real struggle for women in midlife is to "transcend dependency through self-declaration." And, speaking as a woman in midlife, I think having "a thing" helped me achieve that. After all, you can't have the niggling sense you're more than you seem when *who you are* is emblazoned on your T-shirt. And I know self-declaration is a far cry from self-determination, but at least it's a step up from self-care, the substitute aspiration we've been sold. That was the conclusion reached by the writer Anne Helen Petersen too. After researching her book on burnout, she reported that "skincare routines, pedicures, sweet treats, elaborate vacations, even massages—none of it feels as good as actually figuring out something you like to do, and then doing it as if no one was watching, and no one ever will, and it will never, ever find a place on your résumé."

But you know what? Feeling good is only the beginning.

The reason I'm here, the reason I'm telling you all this, is because of what can happen *next*.

I want to show you something. Look.

❤

SAGE HAD JUST MARRIED HER HUSBAND AND WAS ready to start the settle-down-and-have-kids phase of her life with him in Idaho. But then work unexpectedly took her overseas, where, alone and waiting for her husband to join her, she becomes obsessed with *Sherlock*. Then Sage starts getting in touch with feelings she hasn't properly explored before. She finds enormous support in the *Sherlock* community. "I had always wanted to date women, but the thing about being bi is you can always take the route that isn't going to be misunderstood or discriminated against," she tells me. She assumed "fairy-tale" marriage and kids was the next step of her life, "but then I realized, it just wasn't." Sage separates from her husband after five months and meets a wonderful woman, now her wife. She doesn't want kids anymore. "I have everything in my life that I need," she says.

Melissa, from Yorkshire—"but not the nice part"—was at rock bottom when Benedict Cumberbatch turned up, via *Doctor Strange*. She once had dreams of joining the army, but now she was in her thirties, suffering from arthritis and other chronic health conditions. Depressed, and angry at the world, Melissa is surprised to find herself captivated by the character of Stephen Strange. She sees him forging a new future from his own dashed dreams, and something changes in her. "That's what made me think, 'Right, I can still do things; it's just not going to be like how it was before.'" She enrolls in a film studies degree program and finds the energy to do some exercise. It gives her, she tells me, a new reason to live. She sends through a photo of her cosplaying Dr. Strange at the London Comic Con. She's kneeling next to a cute kid dressed as Harry Potter. Usually Melissa can't kneel because of her arthritis, but when the kid asked for a photo, without a moment's hesitation, she put her walking stick to one side and got down on her bad knee. "I don't know what happened," she says. "I forgot all my problems. I became someone else."

Finn had just moved to New York to start their much-anticipated PhD in music cognition, but it wasn't quite the experience they'd been hoping for. They had a lot of pent-up intellectual energy, and Benedict Cumberbatch, somehow, became the perfect outlet for it. So Finn starts studying Benedict Cumberbatch. Like, really, *studying* him: analyzing his performances; scrutinizing his appeal; writing him letters—which read more like essays—about aspects of their research he might be interested in. Finn starts playing around with performing too, recording *Sherlock* podfics, and truly inhabiting Benedict Cumberbatch. They even try smoking, just to see how it feels to hold a cigarette like Sherlock (it doesn't stick). The whole experience "gave me an excuse to express masculinity in a way I hadn't before," Finn says, "and a kind of masculinity which was not at all toxic, that I could relate to much more than the masculinity I'd seen performed around me in other parts of life." They're shocked by how it feels, revealing a deeper understanding of their own trans and nonbinary gender identity. "So much of the fandom experience is more about ourselves than the inspiring objects," Finn says.

Kameo was an empty nester. She'd spent the previous eighteen years as a working single mother, raising a son with special needs. But now she has actual free time and she uses it to become obsessed with *Sherlock*. She launches herself into the world of explicit fanfiction, then decides to try writing the kind of fic she's reading. It's erotic in a kinky, BDSM way, featuring bondage, discipline, dominance, and submission. This is a side of her sexuality she's always known about but been ashamed of, a "dark secret" hidden deep inside her, taboo even to herself. But as an anonymous online fic author, it all comes out. She's proud of the positive feedback she gets from her readers, and this confidence snowballs into courage—the kind of courage a person might need to make their first visit to a BDSM sex club in New York City. And so Kameo, a woman in her fifties, laboring under "decades and decades of shame on top of shame," steps inside. "It expanded my life in a way I would never have imagined," she says. She feels immediately liberated, like "a more intact person." Now she has a new circle of friends, a new partner she met online, and a book deal with an independent publisher for an erotic novel she's written. "My life has changed in such a short period of time, at such a relatively late stage of my life," she says. "It really feels like, *oh*, you just never know what's possible."

Oh, these stories! These wonderful people. And there are so many more too, more people, more stories. I could listen to them all day, and for a time I did. And after each conversation, my cheeks aching from smiling too much, I'd find myself thinking the same question: How is *Benedict Cumberbatch* doing *this*? I mean, Benedict Cumberbatch is incredible, capable of many things, but what appears to be happening here is he's completely changing the lives of those who gaze upon him. And even I can see that's a pretty long bow. No one's cheekbones are that powerful. So, *how*?

❤

I DECIDE TO CALL KAMEO BACK. SHE EXPLAINS THINGS just like a teacher, which is because that's her job, and has been for thirty years. If anyone can offer me an answer, it's Kameo. Besides, I love speaking with her.

I reach her over video call, but the connection is bad, so we turn our cameras off, then both admit we prefer it that way. Who wants to look at themselves? I've taken to sticking a Post-it over the image of my face on my laptop screen, just so I don't have to. Kameo says she feels similarly conflicted about her appearance, describing herself as "not particularly traditionally attractive." This isn't what I called to talk about, but it's what we talk about anyway.

As a child, she says, her father—"bless his heart"—would

point out other girls as being pretty, or adorable, or ladylike. "And I was none of those things, so the message very early on was, 'Good thing I'm smart!'" Growing up, almost all of her identity emanated from this starting point of being clever, not pretty. She diminished people who placed value on their physical appearance or used their looks to get ahead. She opted out of any competition that seemed like it was founded on beauty or femininity. "It was as if I said, 'Go ahead, you take over, I'll be over here in the corner doing a crossword puzzle.'"

"Yes," I say. "I am familiar with this approach." I wore an ugly, baggy suit to my Year 12 formal—the Australian version of the prom—to signal that I had withdrawn my body from consideration. Instead, I threw everything I had at my intellectual identity, the cornerstone of which was the utter disparagement, on ideological grounds, of superficiality and shallowness, and of girls who wore silk formal dresses with spaghetti straps. Kameo says she hasn't worn dresses, unless absolutely necessary, nor makeup, for as long as she can remember. "A lot of preconceived ideas are built on singular experiences a long time ago," she notes. "You lock it up in a box and you don't look at it again." Yes. I am *familiar* with this approach.

When she was a teenager, Kameo says, her home life in Queens was "challenging." She was in a hurry to grow up and move out, which meant always taking the sensible option, like a babysitting job, over the fun ones, like outings with friends. She missed out on many of the typical teenage experiences. She never put herself out there, never took risks. "I feel so terrible for her," she says, remembering the girl she used to be. "Oh, I might cry thinking about it, how scared she was and how alone she was. She was unable to step outside herself and really reach for things that she wanted." Now, she says, "to think of myself as someone who would go to a sex club in New York City to see what it was like . . ." She trails off in disbelief. "It's a whole side of me that I never would have pursued, or even considered, without *Sherlock*." And I remember why I called: Benedict Cumberbatch.

"Surely," I say, "you can't *really* think all of this is attributable to *Sherlock*? Give yourself a bit more credit."

Kameo considers her answer. "No, if it hadn't been for *Sherlock*, I certainly think it's possible I never would have discussed my sexuality—at all," she says. "Maybe there was another path which could have gotten me here, but I can't see it. I really can't."

I shake my head, exasperated. "But it's not a path," I say. "There's no logical connection between the TV show and the sex club."

"But that doesn't matter," Kameo says. I was right about her being good at explaining things.

The TV show, she says, or Benedict Cumberbatch, or whatever, it's just a means to an end. It's not important what it is; it's only important that it makes you feel good. "It's a doorway," she says, and one you can stumble across anywhere, anytime. Maybe even while watching TV. "Then you can either say, '*Yes*, this intrigues me,' step through it, and explore what you find. Or you don't, and you stay stuck where you are."

If you choose to go through the door, she says, you start down a path. It sets off a kind of chain reaction. That's what she found. One thing leads to another. You discover—or maybe you remember—your capacity for feeling good, for having fun. You realize what you're capable of, and you start to exercise that capability, wanting more and more from your life, demanding it, even. That's how it works. "The joy of it expands," she says. It's no longer just to do with a celebrity or a TV show; it's about how you see yourself in the world.

It took me a long time to grasp this, but I think I get it now: something trivial, like a crush on a celebrity, can have unexpected, maybe profound, consequences, not *in spite of* being trivial but *because* it is. Because it's fun, because it doesn't matter, because it's purely for you, because it feels stupidly good. Because the joy of it expands. It seeps into other parts of your life, transforming it, and you, in ways that do matter—a lot. That's why I wasn't able to balance the books between seeing Benedict Cumberbatch in a top hat and what happened next. It's not a one-to-one correlation, but more like an exponential curve. Benedict Cumberbatch can't change your life, you see. But finding your thing, and loving it, whatever it is—well, maybe that can.

"If you suddenly and unexpectedly feel joy, don't hesitate. Give in to it." So says Mary Oliver in her poem "Don't Hesitate." I bought her collected works; I wanted to pay closer attention to what she has to say. And she says there are sources of joy all around us, you just need to embrace them: "Joy is not made to be a crumb." If you tend to that intriguing flicker of *This feels good* or *I want that*, it becomes a flame, bright enough to light your way down previously darkened paths. It's hard to see the final destination when you take the first step, but you'll get there: *This feels like me.*

I laugh, delighted, at Kameo's explanation. She's completely right, and I see now that it's obvious, that it's not about Benedict Cumberbatch at all. Then I tell her some of the stories about other people I've spoken to, and the places their joy has ended up taking them. She's not surprised at all. "I think we know what we're doing without realizing it," she says. "We know what we need. We know where we need to go."

❤

BENEDICT CUMBERBATCH TOOK ME WHERE I NEEDED to go: the spare room. It's not very imaginative, is it? He could have opened any door for me, leading me anywhere, and I chose a *literal* door. But it's what I needed most: a space free from the demands of others, and some time all to myself. I needed to be able to peel back the corner of the motherness, just enough to remind myself what was underneath—what *I* wanted.

And it turned out to be the same thing I always wanted: to write about the things I love. Then one thing led to another, and a fanzine writer finally produced a real publication. We all have somewhere we need to go.

And you? Where might you need to go? I don't want to

tell you what to do, but it might be worth asking yourself the question. I guess a better first question is this: If a door presented itself, would you let yourself step through? And if you can't even imagine that happening, if it seems like there's nothing you love enough, or want enough, don't feel bad about it—you don't need extra things to feel bad about. But if this is the case, then perhaps you could try looking back. Think about something you used to love. It doesn't really matter *what* it was; it's just to remind you what you're capable of, to remember how it feels. Think about what might happen if you felt like that again. I wonder where that could take you? And I know I've made heavy work of all this, but I reckon you'll do a much better job of it. You just have to love something—anything—like your life depends on it. Maybe it does?

It's not always a happy ending, of course. Lea had to shutter her beauty salon in Ohio, after twenty-seven years of business. Isn't that awful? But it couldn't withstand the pandemic. Then one of her Jack Russells passed away, and two others got sick and what good is Benedict Cumberbatch when the vet bills are due? But before COVID, Lea went back to the UK again, her second trip overseas. She saw a play on the West End, starring Andrew Scott. He's Moriarty in *Sherlock* as well as the Hot Priest in *Fleabag*, a character responsible for the ignition of many an internal flicker. When Lea met Benedict Cumberbatch at the *Hamlet* stage door all those years ago, she said she didn't want a selfie because she looks "stupid" in photos. But this time, she took a photo with Andrew Scott. She looks incredible, just beaming.

❤

BENEDICT CUMBERBATCH'S FACE IS EVERYWHERE NOW: my laptop, my phone, my drink bottle, my bag, the fridge. It's totally out of control, and I wouldn't want it any other way. It's like Dulcie with her unicorns, displayed on every available surface, including on everything she wears, from her headbands down to her socks. She even has a unicorn handbag now; it goes perfectly with the glittery pink high heels she got from her uncle for her birthday. He wrapped them in tissue paper, put them in a fancy shoebox, and presented them to her like she was a princess. "They're the highest heels you can get in your size!" he told her, and she was delighted. They're like less than an inch high. I can't believe I ever got so worked up about something so small. The best place to wear them is the supermarket, Dulcie tells me. That's where you get the right click-clack sound.

Kids love unicorns, the theory goes, because *they* choose *you*. They only reveal themselves to those who believe in them. This fosters the hope, the writer Nina Shen Rastogi says, that the unicorn will be "attracted to something ineffable about you, secret from the rest of the world." This is the ultimate fantasy: that "someday you will be recognized as the secretly beautiful, magical thing that you are."

Dulcie wears her unicorns, and I wear Benedict Cumberbatch. I touch my hand to his face on my brooch, my

St. Benedict. Whenever I bend down to tie little shoelaces, or to pick up dirty washing off the floor, I can smell it, the laser-cut wood. It's the smell of the woodwork room from high school—a reminder of the last time in my life when I wore my identity so close to my heart. I breathe it in. *I am still here.* It's a through line, something to hold on to. And maybe I won't love Benedict Cumberbatch forever, and that's okay. I can get a different brooch. It will still feel like me.

Maybe I'll fall for Harry Styles next. It's hard not to. The fangirls feminize him and he welcomes it; it only makes him hotter, the ultimate "big balls move." Teddy and Dulcie love him already. His song "Treat People with Kindness" has become something of a family anthem for us. We have a rule that when it comes on, you have to stop what you're doing and dance. I have danced to that song in the kitchen, wearing a suds-covered apron; in the bedroom, with one sock on, half-dressed for work; and in the supermarket, with Dulcie sparkling under the fluorescent lights, her shoes making exactly the sound she wants to hear.

I started listening to music again; did I mention that? I just felt like I wanted to. Being inside the spare room with Benedict Cumberbatch made it so much better to be outside it. I would open the door and find I was happier to be in the company of my family. I was happier about most things. And angrier too, about the kinds of things that require rage to change. They're on my list of interests now. Knowing what you want is a powerful fuel.

Is it really all thanks to Benedict Cumberbatch? I don't

know for sure, but he showed me the path that got me here. I'm glad I took the first step. It seemed like I was going backward, but it was the right direction after all. Anyway, I just wanted to tell you how good it feels. And that it's worth it. Because it's as clear as anything to me now: this is a book about joy.

this is an appendix about benedict cumberbatch

What's something this book has that Benedict Cumberbatch does not? That's right! An appendix. Benedict Cumberbatch was at the cinema, a twelve-year-old boy watching *Working Girl*, when he started experiencing stomach cramps, and a few hours later, he was at the hospital having an appendectomy. If you look closely (and you know I have) at the *Vanity Fair* cover photo where his thumb is tugging at his waistband, you can see the scar.

The whereabouts of Benedict Cumberbatch's internal organs is exactly the kind of information you'll find in the appendix about Benedict Cumberbatch. But just like Benedict Cumberbatch's actual appendix, it's entirely extraneous; you can choose to read it, or not, depending on just how much you'd *really* like this to be a book about Benedict Cumberbatch.

Notes on chapter one

Benedict Cumberbatch's strange name occupied journalists for whole paragraphs, and sometimes *many* whole paragraphs, early in his career. The author of a 2007 profile in the *Times* can hardly control himself, musing on the name throughout the introduction, the closing line, and even other bits in between. "But it must have been concocted as some kind of joke. Surely?" he asks the man named Benedict Cumberbatch, who is then forced to say, "It's actually my real family name." Benedict Cumberbatch did try to avoid this situation, starting his acting career as Benedict Carlton, following in the footsteps of his father, whose stage name is Timothy Carlton (né Cumberbatch). But his agent recommended he revert to his birth name because "it will get people talking about you." Not always in the ways you want, though. When Stacey Cumberbatch was appointed New York City commissioner of citywide administrative services in 2014, she revealed that the connection between her family and Benedict Cumberbatch was that one of his ancestors owned a plantation in Barbados, where her family was enslaved.

Benedict Cumberbatch's mispronunciation of "penguin" as *pengwing* in the narration for the BBC documentary *South Pacific* was a gift not only for meme-ists but also linguists. It went on to be cited in multiple linguistics textbooks as a "celebrated" example of the phonological process of long-distance assimilation, where we accidentally harmonize sounds in a word. Other examples are the mispronunciations of "orangutan" as *orangutang* (which is so common that this is basically how we pronounce it now), and "smorgasbord" as *smorgasborg*. We have an instinctive urge to make rhymes, linguist Kate Burridge says, plus "in the case of *pengwing* there's the added motivation that the remodeled word nicely captures those rather rudimentary little wings so much a feature of the penguin."

Linguists also love the Benedict Cumberbatch Name Generator! The "Internet Linguist," Gretchen McCulloch, did a great explainer for *The Toast* on how it works on a linguistic level. The key ingredients you need are two words (which can be made up of smaller words), of three syllables each, with a stress on the first syllable. But you also need words that fulfill at least three of the following: they end in a consonant; they begin with *b* or *c*; they end in *s*, *sh*, or *ch*; they have *n* or *m* between the first two syllables; or there's an *æ* sound in the last syllable of the last word. This is why Bendandsnap Calldispatch, Rinkydink Curdlesnoot, and Bumbershoot Cheeseburger all work as stand-ins for Benedict Cumberbatch, but Orangutang Smorgasborg does not.

Being a TV critic, Caitlin Moran had seen *Sherlock* before it aired. Being a person with eyes, she knew what was coming. In an interview with the writer Sara Dobie Bauer, Moran remembers, "When it first broadcast, I was up on Twitter going, 'Women, believe me, you'll want to turn your televisions on in ten minutes.'" Then Moran settled in for a rewatch, drink in hand, so "the first couple tweets were like, 'As you can see, this is a very quality drama.' Then, the third one was like, 'God, he's beautiful.'" And it only got worse/ better from there. Benedict Cumberbatch apparently saw all these tweets as they were happening, and when Moran subsequently had to interview him, she says he looked "slightly nervous." "But he's just so lovely and oddly teenaged," she says. She's interviewed him several times now. "You couldn't find better company if you tried. He's utterly adorable. When you get to know him, you can even call him 'Benny.'"

Benedict Cumberbatch has written about the carjacking experience. "I will always remember that 'How to Disappear Completely' by Radiohead was playing," he says. "This haunting track was halfway through, the window was down, and we were relaxing into the journey. That's when things started to go wrong." Later, believing he was about to be shot, he says, "I thought of home and how, despite being near other people, we all die utterly alone."

Notes on chapter two

At the beginning of his career, Benedict Cumberbatch was, simply, not good-looking. In a *Sunday Times* profile from 2005, the journalist Patricia Nicol writes he has the "wide-eyed features of a meerkat caught on the hop," making him "unlikely to find fame playing pretty boys." I think Nicol underestimated how attractive meerkats are, but also, the reality is that *no one* used to think Benedict Cumberbatch was attractive. "Benedict Cumberbatch's Own Mother Thought He Wasn't Hot Enough to Play Sherlock Holmes" reads a brutal headline in *Vulture*. The BBC agreed, rebuking the *Sherlock* showrunners for their casting: "You promised us a sexy Sherlock, not him." But when Benedict Cumberbatch walked onto the set of 221B Baker Street done up in costume, everything changed. As showrunner Mark Gatiss observed: "He was a weird man a few minutes ago, a sort of ginger weird person. But that disappeared."

Benedict Cumberbatch then became extremely attractive, topping every possible list of the sexiest people alive. "I've grown up with this face and it's been in the industry for ten years," Benedict Cumberbatch said, "and now it's getting on these 'hottie' lists. And I just go, well, it doesn't make any sense because I was nowhere near the one thousandth hottest face when I started out." (It does make me wonder, are we *all* just one very nice coat away from being the sexiest person alive?) The hotness of Sherlock then somehow transferred to Benedict Cumberbatch himself so that even out of costume, we now found him more attractive than we used to. But not all the time. "At certain angles he looks like my aunt," the singer Rufus Wainwright said after working with Benedict Cumberbatch on a Royal Shakespeare Company production, "and then at certain angles he looks like the man who's gonna ruin my marriage."

Benedict Cumberbatch would throw out his dirty napkin, but he's aware of the value of his bodily fluids. In an interview with Jada Yuan for *New York* magazine, Benedict Cumberbatch accidentally gets food on Yuan's phone while they're eating. "Oh, no!" he says. "I've got a bit of ceviche splat on your fucking Samsung. I'm so sorry! Oh, Jesus!" Yuan says it's fine. "Now the phone is worth something." "Exactly," Benedict Cumberbatch says, laughing. "I was going to say, 'Go and frame the phone and sell it on eBay or something.' Though it's not my splat. It's not a Cumbersplat. It's a ceviche splat." The questionnaire did not ask if I would spend several thousand dollars on a Cumbersplat.

Notes on chapter three

Benedict Cumberbatch does not understand being obsessed with Benedict Cumberbatch. When performing *Frankenstein* at the National Theatre, he told the *Telegraph* he would see the same fans in the front row, night after night. "I was like, this is weird. And I told them that, and they were mortified. I said, 'But come on, look, just hear me as one of you. Because I used to be in the audience, I used to obsess about things. But I don't understand this.'"

Characters Benedict Cumberbatch has played who are obsessed with something, but in a male-genius kind of way: Vincent van Gogh (*Van Gogh: Painted with Words*), Alan Turing (*The Imitation Game*), Sherlock Holmes (*Sherlock*), Victor Frankenstein (*Frankenstein*), Julian Assange (*The Fifth Estate*), Stephen Hawking (*Hawking*), and Thomas Edison (*The Current War*).

Benedict Cumberbatch knows about risqué *Sherlock* fan art. Speaking to MTV, he says he's "startlingly aware" of it. It's "all there on the web if you want to find it. I was amazed at the level of artistry," he adds. "I suppose my bodily proportions are quite flattering. I'm ripped, doing something I wouldn't normally do with my body, or having done to it, involving Watson."

Notes on chapter four

In high school, Benedict Cumberbatch was already all about acting. Stephen Fry tells a story in his memoir of how he once judged a reading competition at Harrow, and "awarded one of the schoolboys, who went by the exotic name of Benedict Cumberbatch, second prize. Second." Fry looks upon himself, he says, "as the fisherman who let the big one go." Martin Tyrell, Benedict Cumberbatch's drama teacher, told the *Radio Times* that *he* knew, even at the time, he was witnessing an outstanding talent. "It's probably once in a lifetime that you find a boy actor as magnificent as this. . . . I remember him auditioning very early on for the part of a saucy French maid in a farce. It was a small part, involving a feather duster for about ten minutes." This description doesn't do wonders for what one imagines life is like at a posh British boarding school. Tyrell also apparently called Benedict Cumberbatch's Rosalind in *As You Like It* "the finest since Vanessa Redgrave's" (until his voice broke, he played mostly female roles in school productions). "I have seen pictures of that and it's quite scary," Benedict Cumberbatch later said of his Rosalind. "I look like I am possessed by a woman."

Benedict Cumberbatch also got into music in the nineties. Reminiscing during an interview with *NME*, he says he had magazine posters of Ride, David Bowie, and the Pixies' Frank Black on his walls at boarding school. He was also "big into *NME*" during the era when the newspaper demanded its readers pick a side in the Blur vs. Oasis Britpop war. Benedict Cumberbatch was Team Blur.

Benedict Cumberbatch then studied drama at Manchester University during the latter years of "Madchester"—the city's drug-fueled indie-dance boom—which was something I was reading about, over ten thousand miles away, in my British music magazines. He tells *GQ*'s Stuart McGurk he had a blast—"girls, drinking, clubbing." Pills? McGurk asks. "I was a student in Manchester," Benedict Cumberbatch says with a laugh, by way of an answer. "But, uh, I'll take the Fifth."

Notes on chapter five

Before she was Benedict Cumberbatch's mother, the actress Wanda Ventham was most famous for starring in the seventies sci-fi series *UFO*, but she appeared on many other British TV shows too. "It's Good News to Know I'm Still Fanciable" is the headline of a *TV Times* story about Wanda a year before Benedict Cumberbatch was born. The article mentions that a "high proportion of her fan mail comes from those who like to commit their erotic fantasies to paper"—which turns out to be an inheritable trait! The next time we see Wanda in the *TV Times*, she's photographed in various caftans, pregnant with Benedict Cumberbatch, with the headline "Sex Appeal from a Curvy Mum-to-Be." "I've been trapped with men in elevators who say to me, 'Oh . . . I really used to like your mum. She's really hot,'" Benedict Cumberbatch would say later, once he was born. "I don't know what to say. If I say, 'No, she's not,' that is really insulting to my mother, and if I say she is, it seems very wrong. She is smokin', I guess."

Once she'd had Benedict Cumberbatch, the sexy Wanda Ventham was now a Mother. Even though she kept acting, her press clippings from here on are all about her "domesticated" life. In 1979, when Benedict Cumberbatch is three, she's interviewed by the *TV Times* at the family's Kensington flat. Benedict Cumberbatch is there too, and the journalist describes him as an "energetic handful who was treating the living room like a sports stadium." Wanda says her brain goes to jelly watching over him, adding, "He has been rather vile today, though." The (male) journalist then asks Wanda if she's "raunchy," which is a bit weird, and she replies, "Raunchy doesn't sound at all domesticated," which might be even weirder. But the final paragraph really takes the cake: "And Wanda Ventham, who seems to be rather more disturbing than domesticated, started to make Benedict's tea. When you have a Benedict in the house, you can't just sit around all day looking like Wanda Ventham." I have no idea what that means, but Wanda seems to lean into being Mother after that. When she's supposed to be promoting an episode of

Minder in the *TV Times* a couple years later, she tells a truly exceptional anecdote about a recent family holiday in Greece. Five-year-old Benedict Cumberbatch, she says, "went into the water for a splash around and the elastic on his trunks snapped. When he came back on to the beach we discovered he had been stung very badly—probably by a sea anemone—on a very delicate, personal place. He walked like a cowboy—with his legs wide apart—for about a fortnight."

We know all about how Wanda Ventham used her "free time" as a mother, thanks to a feature called "My Weekend" in something called *Women's Realm*, from when Benedict Cumberbatch is thirteen. Here's a highlight: "Saturday afternoons I'm at the ironing board while Tim [Benedict Cumberbatch's father] sits in front of the TV nibbling away at what I term his 'nursery tea.'" She continues, "For Saturday dinner I usually make meat and loads of vegetables for myself, and perhaps something a bit more interesting for Tim." On Sundays, "even in hot weather my menfolk want the traditional roast meat with roast potatoes. I think if I gave them mashed potatoes there'd be a riot." In the same story, she mentions that her son Ben loves spending time with his two-year-old niece (the daughter of his half sister, Tracy, from Wanda's previous marriage). "I think it's a fallacy that young boys don't like babies. Those of my son's generation definitely do. Their wives will be the lucky ones."

After being hot, and then a mother, Wanda's two identities would eventually coalesce when her son becomes famous. "Stars and Their Hot Moms" is the title of a *People* magazine story from 2014, featuring Hot Mom of Benedict Cumberbatch, Wanda Ventham. This same year, she joins the cast of *Sherlock*, playing Sherlock's mother, alongside her husband, playing Sherlock's father. Showrunner Steven Moffat said of the casting, "The fact is his parents are both actors, really good actors, so it was irresistible." Benedict Cumberbatch says he almost cried when he first saw the episode where he appears with his parents. "My massive motivation in life is to make them proud."

Notes on chapter six

Another Cumberbitch variant I've heard used is Cumberbimbo, but only once, by the American author and "proud Cumberbimbo" MaryJanice Davidson. She even dedicated one of her paranormal romance novels, *Undead and Unwary*, to that "magnificent son of a bitch" Benedict Cumberbatch. "My husband is a very understanding man," she says of the dedication.

    Benedict Cumberbatch usually says only very nice things about his fans. As he told Charlie Rose, "These are very intelligent, smart, driven, independent girls, mainly, but boys as well, and men and women—I do appeal to other generations, I hope." But he hasn't always helped the Cumberbitch reputation. In a 2014 *Out* magazine profile, he managed, in the one interview, to offend so many different subsections of his fanbase, it's genuinely impressive. Describing his appearance at Comic Con, he re-creates a scene of teen hysteria that does no one any favors. Then he's quoted as saying *Sherlock* fans "either want to make John [Watson] into a sort of cute little toy, or me into a cute toy, or we're fucking in space on a bed, chained together." The interviewer agrees, saying fanfiction authors have turned the asexual Sherlock Holmes into a "lustful cock monster," a phrase that would immediately, and proudly, find a home on fan T-shirts. In the same profile, Benedict Cumberbatch also refers to two middle-aged women in flowery dresses who approach him during the interview for a photograph (and which he politely declines) as "the florals over there," a comment that many perceived as ageist. A Danish fan-studies scholar, Dr. Line Nybro Petersen, would later make good use of the term in a research paper called "'The Florals': Female Fans over 50 in *Sherlock* Fandom." In it, a fifty-four-year-old British fan says to Petersen, "I don't know how old you are but I am sure there are things you won't feel any differently about . . . than you did when you were eighteen."

People sending me Benedict Cumberbatch mentions reached absolute fever pitch on the day Benedict Cumberbatch saved a Deliveroo cyclist from being mugged. The cut-through of this story was wild, appearing in every imaginable news outlet, and then, on every single occasion, forwarded to me. It's a great story, though, if you somehow missed it. Benedict Cumberbatch was in London, catching an Uber with his wife, when he saw the attack happening and leaped out. As the Uber driver told the *Sun*: "He stood there instructing them in the street, shouting, 'Leave him alone.' I had hold of one lad and Benedict another. He seemed to know exactly what he was doing. He was very brave. He did most of it, to be honest." "There are real-life heroes out there," Benedict Cumberbatch said in a follow-up story that was then forwarded to me by everyone I know, "and I'm not one of them."

Notes on chapter seven

This is how Benedict Cumberbatch describes the characters in *Sherlock* slash fic, during his unfortunate *Out* magazine interview: "It's always, like, one of them is tired, one comes back from work, the other is horny, a lump appears in his trousers, and then they're at it." He continues, "It's usually me getting it—I'm biting Watson's dog tags." Sounds great! Then the interviewer, a man, wonders if women write slash fic to "remove other women from the picture," and Benedict Cumberbatch, also a man, enthusiastically agrees and decides to contribute his own theory. "I think it's about burgeoning sexuality in adolescence, because you don't necessarily know how to operate that. And I think it's a way of neutralizing the threat, so this person is sort of removed from them as somebody who could break their heart." It's interesting that Benedict Cumberbatch seems to believe fanfiction is written only by adolescents. (According to the Archive of Our Own census, the average age of site users is twenty-five, but the age group with the highest proportion of explicit fic *writers* is forty to forty-nine years.) It's also interesting that Benedict Cumberbatch appears to think slash fic is only for straight girls. (In the same census, the sexuality most represented in slash fandom was bi/pansexuality.) But it's *particularly* interesting that Benedict Cumberbatch thinks fic is about not knowing how to operate your sexual desires.

We have data on fic and sex courtesy of a survey of two thousand fans by the *Three Patch Podcast*. Over 75 percent of survey respondents—almost all of whom identified as either female or a gender minority—said they learned a lot about their own sexual preferences through fic. And about 65 percent said their "solitary sexual activities" have been more satisfying since reading explicit fic. But I think the specific question Benedict Cumberbatch and the *Out* interviewer are puzzling over is the *role* of slash fic in female fantasy. Basically, what do girls want with an erotic story that doesn't have any girls in it?

Well, here's how respondents answered a question on the perspectives they enjoy inhabiting when engaging in "solitary sexual activity" with fandom-inspired sexual fantasy. In other words, *who are they* while fantasizing about, say, for example, Sherlock Holmes biting Dr. Watson's dog tags? And bear in mind that respondents could choose multiple answers:

Forty-seven percent said they enjoy inhabiting the perspective of one particular character in the relationship; 25 percent said they prefer the perspective of the more dominant person in the scene and 52 percent the more submissive person. Twenty percent enjoy the perspective of the character portrayed as closest to their gender identity, while 41 percent prefer the character closest to their personality, and 13 percent said it was the character closest to their physical attributes. Fifty-eight percent said they enjoyed the perspective of an outsider observing the scene, and 20 percent inserted themself into the action.

I don't know about you, but it sounds to me like these fic readers know how to "operate" their sexuality. Also, if you think the appeal of slash fic is that it "removes women from the picture," you're kind of forgetting that, if anything, it's (cisgender) men who've been removed from the picture. It's almost entirely women and gender minorities who are in charge of the show.

Notes on chapter eight

Benedict Cumberbatch himself has a problem with seeming, an occupational hazard for an actor. He's played a lot of geniuses, which, he says, just makes him *seem* clever. "Perversely, I am probably one of the stupidest actors I know," he told *Stellar* magazine. "I'm playing some of the smartest characters because I'm drawn to them. They are so different from me." I don't know about this; he seems clever enough. He's definitely well read. "You would have to be a pretty smart cookie to keep up with him," his half sister, Tracy, told the *Sun* back when he was single, and then she followed up with a real zinger: "I think that is why possibly he has trouble with girlfriends." Incredible. But it's easy to confuse the actor with the character. When doing press about his role as Alan Turing, Benedict Cumberbatch had to repeatedly point out that he personally got a B in high school math. When he played Stephen Hawking, one journalist asked him how stars are created. "Good grief, that's a really unfair question," he replied. The entire promotional cycle for *The Grinch* became focused on whether Benedict Cumberbatch hates Christmas (he doesn't, but he *does* hate plastic packaging). After playing Dr. Stephen Strange, Benedict Cumberbatch's co-star Tilda Swinton jokingly asked him if he was confident to answer the call for a neurosurgeon during an in-flight emergency. "Yeah, I could definitely scrub up in the little airplane loo," he says. "I'd get one of those plastic knives out, a few serviettes, and just get carving. It's all very simple once you've opened it up." Benedict Cumberbatch was proud, however, to report some cowboy skills did rub off on him after playing a rancher in *The Power of the Dog*. While on holiday with his family on the Isle of Wight, he found himself among a group of people whose path to the beach was blocked by a herd of cows. "There were people standing there with boogie boards and picnic bags looking terrified because they just wouldn't move," he says. "So I just went, 'I know what to do!' and started herding the cows out of the way."

The biggest-seeming problem for Benedict Cumberbatch came from playing Sherlock Holmes. Benedict Cumberbatch says the closest he gets to being able to do a Holmesian deduction is seeing someone on the train and noticing they have mud on their shoe. And yet, we still want him to be

Sherlock. Comedy writer John Finnemore captures this in a short skit he produced for BBC radio called "What's Benedict Cumberbatch Really Like?" In it, a woman approaches Finnemore and, knowing he worked with Benedict Cumberbatch on *Cabin Pressure*, wants the inside scoop. "Oh, he's down-to-earth, very funny, great to be around," Finnemore replies, but the woman isn't happy with that answer. "But what's he *really* like?" she keeps asking, over and over, as Finnemore searches for increasingly generic descriptions of Benedict Cumberbatch: "He's an adult Caucasian male, above-average height, mild wear on upper-right molars." Then: "He's an omnivorous bipedal mammal." But the woman still isn't satisfied. "But what's he *really* like?" she keeps asking, until Finnemore eventually says Benedict Cumberbatch is just like Sherlock Holmes, a high-functioning sociopath who lives on Baker Street. "You know what?" she replies excitedly. "That is *exactly* how he comes across on the telly!" Benedict Cumberbatch knows this, that he's been typecast. He reports that at a pre-Oscars party, Ted Danson screamed across the room, "Oh my God! Fuck! It's Sherlock! You're Sherlock! Oh God!" He says he consoles himself with the fact that "no one calls George Clooney 'Doug Ross' anymore."

The best confusion between Benedict Cumberbatch and his character comes from Benedict Cumberbatch himself. When a journalist from *Elle* says she thinks Sherlock Holmes wouldn't be any good in the sack, Benedict Cumberbatch vehemently disagrees. "I would be *devastating*," he says, forgetting his pronouns. "I'd know *exactly* how to please a woman, I'd know exactly where to put my fingers, where to put my tongue, where to put my—his, I should say—his fingers, his tongue." Benedict Cumberbatch knows he's mixing up the actor and the character, but he can't stop. "I'd know exactly how to get that person into it, and get pleasure out of making that person feel pleasure to the point that I probably wouldn't even have to enter . . . But when I did"—and in this moment, it seems Benedict Cumberbatch and Sherlock Holmes are one and the same—"it would be explosive." I think Benedict Cumberbatch might understand more about fanfiction than he realizes.

Notes on chapter nine

Benedict Cumberbatch appeared in a sex scene with Scarlett Johansson, early in his film career, in *The Other Boleyn Girl.* And what did his girlfriend at the time think about that? "We had a giggle about it," he told the *Times.* "She was fine."

Feelings about celebrities aren't always benign. Benedict Cumberbatch says he's aware of some "obsessive, deluded, really scary" fan behavior, referring to people online who claim his wife is a criminal mastermind or an escort or something (it's hard to keep up), and his children are all fake. It's the kind of thing that has been going on since Paul McCartney supposedly died in a car crash in the sixties, but now with added internet.

On the subject of Benedict Cumberbatch's objectification, Caitlin Moran asked him if he'd be happy, in the interests of feminism, to "play a role in a female-centered film where you were man-totty? Hot, objectified manmeat?" He replies cheerfully, "If it's good enough for Chris Pine [in *Wonder Woman*], it's good enough for Benedict Cumberbatch! Yeah! Definitely!" Moran suggests he'd appear only in his underpants, in a slow pan from feet to the head, and Benedict Cumberbatch chimes in, ". . . with sexy screaming saxophone music in the background? Ha-ha-ha, yes! So long as it was fun. I'd have to be in good shape, though. Prepare."

If you would like to objectify Benedict Cumberbatch in the truest possible sense of the word, breaking him down to his component parts, you're in luck—someone has already done it for you. As Bill Bryson reports in his book *The Body*, the Royal Society of Chemistry has worked out not only every precise element contained in the body of Benedict Cumberbatch—mostly carbon, oxygen, hydrogen, nitrogen, calcium, and phosphorus—but also exactly how much it would cost you to buy these elements if you wanted to build your own Benedict Cumberbatch at home from scratch (£96,546.79, not including VAT or cost of construction).

Benedict Cumberbatch understands the patriarchy and his role in it. In the same interview with Caitlin Moran in which he says he's happy to be manmeat, Benedict Cumberbatch announced that he won't take a role unless the female actors on the project are being paid the same as the men. He's proud that he and his friend Adam Ackland are the only men employed by his production company SunnyMarch. "If it's centered around my name, to get investors, then we can use that attention for a raft of female projects." When he was asked in a later interview—in which he's supposed to be promoting luxury watches—about what it means to be a modern "gentleman," he replied, like a goddamn gentleman, it's "about passing that platform on to other people."

Top 10 Benedict Cumberbatch characters, hairwise, according to me: 1. Sherlock Holmes (*Sherlock*); 2. Sherlock Holmes (the different hair he has in "The Abominable Bride" special); 3. Wallace ("Little Favour"); 4. King Richard III (*Richard III*); 5. Christopher Tietjens (*Parade's End*); 6. Prince Hamlet (*Hamlet*); 7. Stephen Lewis (*The Child in Time*); 8. William Prince Ford (*12 Years a Slave*); 9. Stephen Strange (*Doctor Strange*); 10. Little Charles (*August: Osage County*).

The worst hair is surely Dominic Cummings (*Brexit: The Uncivil War*), which was so bad that whenever he wasn't on set, Benedict Cumberbatch had to wear a hat, including to accept his South Bank Sky Arts Outstanding Achievement Award. "I'm not wearing this to remain aloof and anonymous," he explains on stage, but because of the "horror story that is my haircut." Notable mention goes to the Julian Assange platinum blond bob for *The Fifth Estate*. When that movie came out, the singer Phoebe Bridgers wasn't famous. But as soon as she was, it was pointed out how much she looked like Benedict Cumberbatch looking like Julian Assange. She embraced it, selling a T-shirt on her 2018 tour that was, simply, a photo of Benedict Cumberbatch as Assange, printed beneath the words "Phoebe Bridgers." Amazing.

Benedict Cumberbatch's face has appeared on more than one birthday cake. The actress Keeley Hawes told a great story about this on *The Graham Norton Show*. She says while she was filming *The Hollow Crown* somewhere in the British countryside, she went out to dinner at a local pub with co-stars Benedict Cumberbatch and Dame Judi Dench. A few pubgoers noticed these celebrities in their midst and were checking them out, but then a sixteen-year-old girl came up to them and started to cry. "*Sobbing!*" Hawes says. "And it turned out that she was having, in the hall next door, in the middle of nowhere, a Benedict Cumberbatch–themed birthday party—with the cake with Ben's face on it—and *there he was*! With Judi Dench as a sort of side note. It was quite extraordinary. It was a wonderful thing to see. And of course he was brilliant, because he's lovely." Graham Norton adds, "Isn't that terrible, when your life has peaked at sixteen."

Notes on chapter ten

Benedict Cumberbatch was already at boarding school when the *Police Academy* movies were released. They probably didn't show them there. "I was never obsessive about anything I watched when I was a kid," he told *SFX* magazine, "except maybe *The A-Team* and *Airwolf*. . . . And I loved *Knight Rider* and *Baywatch*. But I was never obsessed." He was eight when he was sent away to school, which he says, "seems a bit of a wrench. I don't know if I could do it with a kid of eight." He has a recurring dream, he told *Harper's*

Bazaar, where he's been abandoned in his grandmother's house and wakes up to find everyone's gone. "So speaks a child who went to boarding school." He laughs. "Abandonment issues, I think that could be it. I forgive you, Mum and Dad. It's fine." In a later interview he'd clarify his feelings about the experience, saying, "The first lump-in-the-throat moments were really horrible, but they were soon overridden by the sheer joy of what I was doing. It was like a band of brothers: sailing and camps and cricket and boys being boys and having adventures." He's now the father to three young sons, his own "very merry band."

Benedict Cumberbatch's wife, theater director Sophie Hunter, was obsessed with the English pop band Bros when she was a teenager. Benedict Cumberbatch manages to reveal this information while being interviewed on the red carpet at the BAFTA Awards one year. As soon as the words leave his lips, you can see the flash of realization on his face that he has said The Wrong Thing. "She's going to hate me for saying that!" he says, shaking his head, and smiling straight down the lens, a man resigned to his fate. For his part, the first record Benedict Cumberbatch bought was *Now That's What I Call Music!: Volume 24* featuring 2 Unlimited, Shaggy, and Duran Duran.

Notes on chapter eleven

Benedict Cumberbatch has many interests. He reads a lot (a bit of a literary critic himself, he once did book reviews for

British TV chat show *Richard & Judy*) and likes music (Sigur Rós, Radiohead, Elbow, Pink Floyd, David Bowie). He swims, he writes, he practices his French, he supports many excellent causes (including appearing at an Extinction Rebellion protest), he goes to Wimbledon, he talks about how he's vegan or not vegan, he does yoga and meditates. But his "thing" is clearly acting, and always has been, well before it was his profession. "I really, really love my job," he told *Vogue*. "I love sets. I love crews. I love theaters. I love *audiences*." In the lead-up to his run as Hamlet, Benedict Cumberbatch was asked if he was preparing for the role, and he replied, "I started preparing for Hamlet when I was seventeen. Probably before that." He has always loved the one thing, and has never stopped. When he appeared in *A Midsummer Night's Dream* at the age of twelve, the title of the review in the school magazine prophesied everything to come: "Benedict Cumberbatch's Bottom Will Long Be Remembered."

Benedict Cumberbatch has his own sense of what's weird and what's normal. Speaking with Claire Foy in a *Variety* "Actors on Actors" video, he says about meeting fans, "The selfie thing is a bit weird. I do still feel like, Can we not just have a moment? Can we not just say hello? I don't want a selfie with, I don't know, Paul McCartney. I want to talk to him. I want to talk to him about chord structures, albums, tours, you know what I mean? Dig a bit deeper." Some things are normal (talking about chord structures), some things are weird (photos of bone structure). We'll have to agree to disagree. Benedict Cumberbatch then says that Claire Foy must have the same problem with fame now, being so recognizable from *The Crown*. "I'm really fortunate, in the sense that I have always—" And she stops herself, starts again. "*You*," she says to Benedict Cumberbatch, "are a very distinctive-looking person." "I'm an odd-looking person," he says, and Claire Foy, horrified, says, "No! It's not about being odd-looking!" and he says, "But I am. Me and Matt Smith, you can kind of spot us." In contrast, Claire Foy says she can walk into a room and people will squint at her, thinking, "'Hmm, did I work with her? Is she my cousin?' I'm familiar to people, but I don't *attract* attention."

There aren't many occasions when you get to cheer for an actor like they're your sports team, but when Benedict Cumberbatch won his first BAFTA TV Award after six previous nominations, I was legitimately elated. I actually leaped up and punched the air, which isn't a thing I do. Having never followed a sport of any kind, it was educational: you really *can* experience someone else's victory as your own! A Canadian friend once told me that ice hockey fans riot after a loss, but riot *even more* after a victory, and now that made perfect sense. I was all set to flip a car and light something on fire. That the win was for *Patrick Melrose* made it even better. It is, in my opinion, the best performance of Benedict Cumberbatch's career, my absolute favorite. If you—and is this even possible?—have gotten this far into this book without having seen Benedict Cumberbatch in anything, maybe you could start here.

Notes on chapter twelve

Denigrating their own looks is something many of the Cumberbitches do in my conversations with them. I heard the phrase "I'm not exactly a model myself" so many times, unprompted, it became really unsettling. Benedict Cumberbatch will similarly never pass up an opportunity to talk down his appearance. On the subject of his resemblance to an otter, he says, "It's a great disservice to a wonderful woodland amphibious creature." I wonder, does this somehow make him more attractive to women who are unhappy with their own looks? I don't know, but it makes for an interesting dynamic. On one occasion, a fan presented him a photo for an autograph and Benedict Cumberbatch duly signed his name on the image of himself in a tuxedo, seated on a stool, but then scrawled underneath: *Posh Aliens have landed!! HATE this photo . . . Ah well!!* This personalized photo eventually ended up on the r/Cumberbitches subreddit for all to see. "Would still bang," the first commenter declares. "No hesitation," chimes in the next.

Benedict Cumberbatch is in the business of transformations. It's his job to become someone else. When he was preparing to play Dominic Cummings in *Brexit*, he went over to Cummings's house, which you'd think would be very awkward, with them being on opposite ends of the political spectrum. But the *Spectator*'s Mary Wakefield, who is also Cummings's wife, described what happened as "a hell of a thing." "He sat down opposite Dom at about 8.30 p.m. that summer evening in what I imagine is a very Cumberbatchian pose: legs folded beneath him, alert, leaning forward, head up. 'Just water, please, I don't really drink.' By 10:30 he was leaning back, just like Dom, glass of red in hand. By 1 a.m. he was a mirror image of his subject. It was a Rorschach blot of a scene. Both men reclining, each with an arm behind their head." Later, when photos of Benedict Cumberbatch as Cummings appear in the press, Wakefield shows them to her son, and he thinks Benedict Cumberbatch is his father. The two men look nothing alike. "Cumberbatch doesn't so much throw himself into each role as get sucked into them," writes *GQ*. It renders him, *Vanity Fair* says, "a kind of imaginary dress-up doll." He can be whatever you want him to be.

Harry Styles and Benedict Cumberbatch have appeared in public together once, as teammates in a USA vs. UK celebrity dodgeball match on *The Late Late Show with James Corden*. After a shot from Michelle Obama hits Harry Styles "right in the 1D," Benedict Cumberbatch lobs a ball directly at the former First Lady, and is genuinely, and extremely, mortified by what he's done.

Benedict Cumberbatch once opened a door for a sparrow. It's described in *Vanity Fair*. The bird is trapped in the hotel lobby where Benedict Cumberbatch is being interviewed, so he gets up and props open the terrace door with a rubber wedge. It's a nice thing to do—I'd expect nothing less of him—but it doesn't have to mean anything. "After all, what am I? I'm just a cipher for the culture," Benedict

Cumberbatch said on a podcast once. "I'm not that important." We don't always have to make too much meaning. Sometimes Benedict Cumberbatch is a catalyst for profound personal change, guiding us through metaphorical doorways; sometimes he's just a man, opening a door for a bird. But by God, what a man.

acknowledgments

Thank you to all the people who helped me write this book, but especially everyone who entrusted their stories to me, including those whose stories didn't end up on the page. Thank you for being so open, generous, and wise. The book would not exist without you.

Thank you to my agent, Catherine Drayton, who somehow knew what this book was about before I did. And thanks also to both Catherine Milne and Michelle Howry, and their teams at HarperCollins Australia and Putnam, respectively, for their unfaltering support, trust, and enthusiasm from the get-go.

This book began as an essay for *MUTHA Magazine*, and I am hugely grateful to Meg Lemke for publishing it, and for allowing me to include some parts from it in here. The quotes from my interviews with Dr. Liana Leach and Professor Naomi Langmore previously appeared on the Science at

ANU website and are republished with permission of the Australian National University, Dr. Leach, and Professor Langmore. The fanfiction extract that appears in chapter seven comes from the story "whiskies neat" and is used with the kind permission of the author, Ellipsical.

Thank you to Jo Sharpe, Amanda Cox, Jimmy Walsh, Dr. Andrea Waling, Karen Gould, Alex Topfer, Sophie Harper, Jen Pinkerton, Mary Cunnane, Alex O'Sullivan, Joe Edwards, Simon Mahood, Nigel De Luis, Nathan James, Ginger Gorman, Amber Dickson, Adam Thompson, everyone at the ACT Writers 2019 HARDCOPY Program, the ANU College of Science, and all my family and friends.

For years and years of feedback and encouragement, my heartfelt thanks to Kate Rowe, Justyna Krzywicka, and Beck Redden.

To Beth Taylor, for everything, always and forever.

To Amber Carvan, for walking alongside me every step of the way, always knowing the right thing to say, and the best thing to do.

And to Nathan, Teddy, and Dulcie: we did it! I love you!

about the author

Jimmy Walsh Photography

Tabitha Carvan is a writer from Canberra, Australia. *This Is Not a Book about Benedict Cumberbatch* is her first book.